Dictionary of Annual Plants

Dictionary of Annual Plants

H. G. Witham Fogg

DRAKE PUBLISHERS INC.

NEW YORK

ISBN 87749-228-X

Published in 1972 by
Drake Publishers Inc
381 Park Avenue South
New York, N.Y. 10016

Library of Congress Catalog Card Number: 74-188801

© H. G. Witham Fogg, 1972

Printed in Great Britain

Contents

List of Illustrations

Foreword

Annual flowers are undoubtedly among the most rewarding plants we can grow in our gardens and no one need be without them. They vary greatly in height from an inch or two to six or seven feet, and the majority are of very simple cultivation.

The main purpose of this book is to provide the flower lover with a concise and practical guide to the use and cultivation of a very large number of plants that produce a wealth of colour in a comparatively short time after seed is sown.

The nomenclature of the species and varieties is based on the code recommended by the International Code of Nomenclature. The fact that some annuals have more than one name is not ignored and this includes the common names which are different in various parts of the country. Reference is also made to some Latin names familiar to gardeners but now regarded as invalid by botanists.

This work is based on personal experience during many years of practical work in horticulture. This has been supplemented by a close connection with seed firms and plant growers, as well as acquaintance with raisers in many parts of the world. I have, therefore, had excellent opportunities to continually increase my knowledge of annual plants and to remain up to date and forward looking.

No aspect of the growing of annuals has been overlooked, so that whether one is using a small bed, a large border or a greenhouse, or is keen on exhibiting, clear guidance is given, as it is in the recognition and treatment of possible pests and disorders.

One

Introduction to Annual Plants

It is a known fact that when the need for food, clothing and housing have been satisfied human beings like to have things of beauty around them. From this springs the desire of the majority of people to grow flowers. This is clearly seen on the new housing estates when almost all occupants attempt to do something to introduce growing plants, and even those without any garden, often plant window boxes, hanging baskets or pots and bowls.

While trees, shrubs and perennial plants form the framework of gardens of all sizes, it is annual plants that will provide a gay and colorful display from spring to autumn quickly, easily and without great expense. There are also tall growing annual foliage plants which will act as temporary screens against walls and fences. These too, where desired, can be used as a background for the more colorful subjects.

Annuals come from various parts of the world, some are natives of Europe, many are found in North and South America, Asia and Australasia, and all parts of Africa. The latter, not unnaturally, are at their very best during warm sunny weather. As a rule all annuals should be kept out of the shade, since in the absence of light, such as under the shade of trees and hedges, the plants become drawn, sappy and weak. Annuals respond to good treatment. They do *not* give best results in poor soil, which is sometimes advocated for them.

Although good cultivation is always advisable, a creditable show can be secured with the minimum of labour. It is possible to obtain a bright display by simply sprinkling seed on the surface of weed-free soil and raking it in. Many half hardy annuals native of South America,

Mexico and South Africa can be raised in boxes in the frame or greenhouse, the plants being moved to their flowering positions in the spring. For this, high temperatures are not needed. They require to be gradually hardened off before they are planted outdoors for the summer. They are usually spoiled as soon as the first autumn frosts of any severity touch them.

All who have seen the magnificent annual borders that have been laid out in the great botanical gardens will know how delightful can be the effect given by such easily raised plants. It is perhaps when annuals are grown in borders by themselves that they are seen at their best, though this is not always practicable or even desirable in small gardens.

Particularly when one is taking over a new garden, hardy annuals are most useful for producing a good effect in a short time and will give color until new borders can be planted with permanent subjects later. Annuals are most effective when arranged in bold groups rather than sprinkled in small quantities or sown in straight lines. The hardy kinds can be sown where they are to flower.

Another point in favour of annuals is that different varieties can be grown each year, so that there is no question of monotony, which can occur with perennials when they are left in position for a long period.

What is an annual? It is a plant which completes its life cycle from germination to seed production within a period of twelve months. In some cases the whole process may take only 5 or 6 weeks. This means that with the right selection it is possible to secure a colorful display in a short time.

Hardy annuals will withstand a certain amount of cold. The half hardy species are susceptible to damage by frost, the degree varying with different plants. Tender or greenhouse annuals require warmer conditions than those provided by our climate and are therefore unsuitable for cultivation outdoors.

If annuals have a short life most of them compensate us by their ease of cultivation and the magnificence of the display they give.

Today new varieties are regularly being introduced and we owe much to the patience and skill of plant breeders in all parts of the world who, by their detailed work, are constantly creating new strains. Strength of growth, size of flowers, increase in color range, length of stem and general improvements in constitution are continually being made. The fact that seed of new varieties is rather more expensive than the older sorts is an indication that plant breeding and selection can be a costly business. It, therefore, follows that seed of new subjects must be sold at a higher price than the older strains of which seed is more plentiful.

The last few years have seen a striking advance in seed production which is usually referred to as heterosis or hybrid vigour. This theory has been known for many years and seed culturists did much work on tomatoes, while Lilium auratum were also used in perfecting the process. The term F.1 hybrid is now used by breeders to signify heterosis in the progeny of two distinct plants. The seed produced from this progeny will not re-produce the characteristics of the parents. The *same* original parents must be crossed every time. There can be no mother seed.

About 15 years ago cucumber, Butcher's Disease Resisting, was crossed with an undisclosed variety and resulted in the F.1 hybrid Market Cross. It was discovered after extensive trials, that if a certain two varieties of tomatoes were crossed, they would produce the F.1 hybrids. The first of these were called Ware Cross and Hertford Cross. Now it is possible to obtain seeds of these F.1 hybrids in many popular flowers including: ageratum, antirrhinum, asters, annual dianthus, marigolds, petunias, salpiglossis and zinnias.

It has been noticed that the crossing of certain varieties produces in the first generation special qualities which are lost in succeeding generations if the hybridist endeavours to fix the result of his original cross. Notable amongst these special qualities are hybrid vigour and earliness, combined with complete uniformity of habit, color, size, form and disease resistance. Certain crosses result in sterility.

The production of large quantities of hybrid seed is an expensive business. It is a delicate, and somewhat tedious job which has to be done at the precise moment. Collection of pollen from the male parent is sometimes done with the aid of an electric bee. It also calls for knowledge and care, while isolation is imperative if true hybrids are to be produced, so that pollen-proof cages are used for crops not grown under glass.

Seeds of annuals vary tremendously in color, size, shape and weight. The following is a list giving the approximate number of seeds to the ounce, of some of the most popular subjects. In certain instances different varieties of the same family have bigger and heavier seeds than others and the figures given are the average.

Ageratum	214,000	Nasturtium	175–250
Antirrhinum	210,000	Petunias	160–250,000
Asters	12,000	Phlox drummondi	18,000
Calendula	3,500–4,500	Poppies	450,000
Cosmea	3–5,000	Salvia splendens	7,500
Cuphea	7,000	Schizanthus	45,000
Godetia	40,000	Stocks	18,500
Gourds—small sorts	500	Sweet Peas	340
Helichrysum mixed	45,000	Thunbergia	830
Hunnemannia	7,000	Tithonia	4,000
Ipomaea	650–850	Ursinia	16,000
Larkspur	8,500	Verbena	12,000
Linaria	460,000	Zinnia dahlia flowered	3,000
Marigolds	8–10,000	Zinnia other types	3–5,000

Certain varieties of the same species do vary considerably in color, size and weight, examples being petunias and zinnias.

Natural Distribution of Seeds

Plants are stationary objects, and there is in the plant world, a great struggle for existence. It is, therefore, necessary for seeds to be distributed as far as possible from the parent plants, so as to give at least a proportion of the seeds a good chance to find suitable conditions for germination. Very many more seeds than are required to carry on plant life are regularly produced, since so many are lost from various causes. It is important that those that do survive, are widely distributed, in order that they come to maturity without harm.

The fact that annual seeds *are* widely distributed by various natural means, can be clearly seen on the flowering derelict sites of cities. Plants of annuals have grown there which have never previously been seen in those neighbourhoods. It is no uncommon sight to see plants growing on old ruins, churches and walls, so that it is certain that the seed was carried to these places by wind or other natural methods. One of the marvels of nature is that seed of some subjects will, under certain conditions, remain viable for many years. There are instances of lobelia, antirrhinums, etc. germinating on being brought near the surface after remaining buried deeply for years.

While there are many ways by which nature arranges for the spread of the seed, the chief methods are:

(a)   Scattering by wind and water. Many seeds are specially equipped with wings or a pappus of hairs, making it easy for them to float through the air. In other instances, such as with poppies and antirrhinums, where the seed is small, it is forced out of the seed capsules or boxes and scattered widely. Rain will splash seeds over wide areas, and of course rising and flood waters often carry seeds many miles.

The wild oat and ornamental grass families have a built in propeller, a black tail, which is tightly wound up. When wet, this tail uncoils and turns the seed round with the pointed end down, so that a rain will induce the seed to plant itself in the moist earth, where it soon takes root and grows.

Some seeds have an 'airforce arm' and are regularly picked up at altitudes up to 5,000 ft. (1 mile high). They can float for great distances. There is a nautical force of seeds which float on rivers and streams, often to a lake where they are released into controlled channels and find their ways into farmers' fields. They are also hitch hikers which catch onto animals, people, moving vehicles and birds, often crossing national boundaries.

(b)   Scattering by explosive fruits. Some flowers bear seed boxes or fruits which, when they become dry, contract and eject the smooth seeds, often throwing them a considerable distance. Notable examples are the oxalis, sweet peas and broom.

(c)   Scattering by adhering to animals. Some seeds are rough or have hooks or little spikes by which they easily cling to the hair or wool of animals by which means they are often carried great distances. In addition, seeds are frequently unknowingly buried by animals which burrow, such as rabbits and squirrels.

(d)   Scattering by being eaten by animals or birds, by which means they are sometimes carried long distances.

A great deal still remains to be found out about seeds and their habits of germination. Most of the knowledge we have to-day consists of facts collected from experience and observation.

A seed is really a young plant, with some food for its early life enclosed with a protective covering. Until germination occurs, the young plant is dormant, and there are considerable differences between the various kinds in the length of the dormant period that can be allowed without loss of vitality. Another big variation lies in the method of advance food storage. In some seeds the young plant absorbs the store of food before becoming dormant, so that it is quite large and swollen. An example is the easily recognisable wound-up embryo that everybody will have seen inside a bean.

Seeds can put up with severe conditions to a remarkable extent. They have been successfully germinated after artificial exposure to very many degrees of frost, and after treatment with boiling water although one would not knowingly allow the latter to occur.

All seed-bearing plants aim to reproduce themselves from seed. If, for some reason, a plant is broken or damaged in any way, it will make every effort to produce seeds before it dies. Very often when rooting conditions are unsuitable, plants run to seed before they are fully grown. In the case of annuals that are damaged, these will remain in growth long after their normal span and as if in desperation they produce flower after flower.

To discover what a seed is, we must begin with its origin, that is pollenation. Apart from the sepals and petals, a flower mainly consists of the anthers which have the pollen sacs at the top and are the male parts, and the stigma, which is the female organ. Many plants are so designed to make self-pollenation difficult, impossible in some cases, while in others, nigella for instance, to force self-pollenation if cross-pollenation fails.

Pollen grains are distributed by wind, insects or chance. When they reach the stigma which is sticky, the grains adhere easily and the next step is fertilisation. In this process the grains send down through the pistil, long tubes which eventually reach the ovary. Subsequently the ovaries become seeds which in turn become individual plants with their own characteristics.

Within the seed coat or testa there are one or two seed leaves or cotyledons and the embryo, which consists of the radicle or root growth, and what will eventually become the stem. The number, weight and shape of seeds makes an interesting study. An ovary may ripen into a seed box containing few or many, in some cases the number runs into thousands. Sometimes the seed box is divided into several compartments.

Some seeds will tolerate amazingly low temperatures. In fact, it has been found that exposure to successive heat and cold treatment increases germination ability. Soft coated seeds germinate more quickly than those with a hard coat because of the ease with which moisture can penetrate the coat. This accounts for the gardener's practice of abrading or even chipping seeds such as sweet peas since such action speeds the germination process.

The making of a seed bed fine and firm is largely bound up with this question. Seed cannot absorb moisture as quickly from soil as when it is immersed in water, but the closer the contact with the earth, the greater the possibility of absorption.

Air and warmth are other requirements for germination. The temperature at which germination occurs will, naturally, vary with the place origin of the plant. Seeds from semi-tropical parts will need a temperature of 70°F or more, while those from the temperate lands will germinate at 40°F. Most seeds germinate well in darkness, but a few prefer the light and therefore need no covering.

The geographical distribution of annuals is of more than passing interest for there are species in all five continents growing naturally under widely different conditions of temperature and environment. However the majority are to be found in the more temperate parts of the world and adapt very easily to be transplated to the countries with similar conditions. Careful cultivation over a number of years can also enable plants from very different climatic backgrounds to become acclimatised and to flourish in these temperature zones.

Native to South America are such lovely plants as petunias, salpiglossis, schizanthus and tropaeolums. One can hardly begin to enumerate the number of excellent varieties that blossom in the gardens of North America; these include such favourites as clarkia, godetia, nemophila and eschscholzia.

South Africa has many composites or daisy-like plants, such as the brilliant arctotis, dimorphotheca, mesembryanthemum, ursinia and venidium.

Subjects which come from the warmer parts of the world almost always are of more brilliant coloring than those from low temperature areas. This, in part, is due to the necessity to attract pollenating insects to the flowers which have such a comparatively short life; flowers from cooler places last longer with more opportunities for the pollenating process to take place.

China and Japan are the homes of *Callistephus hortensis*, from which

16

have come the many forms of the plant we know best as asters.

Mexico is the home of many annuals including numerous forms of tagetes, or marigolds, and tithonia, while in the Mediterranean regions originated a host of plants including Lathyrus odoratus, the sweet pea, in its great variety.

In the Baltic states are to be found a number of popular annuals including papavers. Celosia is a native of India. Australia has produced a number of useful plants, notably the everlastings, helpterums, and helichrysums.

Candytuft Choice Mixed

While much has been done in the selecting and improving of strains received from many different countries, it is the result of the work of plant breeders that so many first class garden hybrids are available to-day. Fortunately, the work continues and when we consider how plants such as antirrhinums, agrostemmas, asters, papavers, sweet peas and zinnias have been improved we can look forward to similar improvements in other well known subjects as well as to, the introduction of even more species.

What has happened in the past can certainly occur again, for there are still many undiscovered treasures growing wild in little known parts of the world. The plant breeder is persistent and consistent in his aims of introducing and improving plants for the benefit and pleasure of everyone.

These facts combined with the great interchange of information between so many countries must lead to further advances. The ability and desire of so many people to travel widely, thereby providing more opportunity of discovering hitherto little known plants, makes the future rosy for the introduction of more and more reliable annuals to furnish our gardens with grace and color.

Two

General Cultivation

Although annual plants are easy to cultivate and have no fussy requirements, the final effect will be reflected in the quality of the flowers produced. Plants seen flowering in spaces between herbaceous plants or among shrubs will provide colourful blooms at a time when the borders might otherwise be somewhat dull and uninteresting.

The quickness of their growth makes them invaluable for giving a temporary display which could not otherwise be provided. The majority of annuals are excellent for cutting, lending themselves readily to decoration arrangements.

Many annuals are first class for window boxes where they will give brilliance in places which would otherwise be dull. Good drainage is essential, and the boxes require a considerable amount of watering especially in dry weather.

In hanging baskets too, annuals are most effective. First line the basket with sphagnum moss and then put in the compost. Seed can be sown directly into the baskets or plants can be raised elsewhere and transplanted once they can be handled easily.

Wherever annuals are cultivated, the selection made should be suitable for the place in which they are to be grown. Species vary in height from 2 in to 6 ft, some being compact, others of spreading habit.

To save taking all the colour from the flower garden, subjects being grown specially for cutting can be sown in groups in odd corners, even in the kitchen garden, and in spaces left bare after early flowering plants such as winter pansies, Canterbury Bells and Sweet Williams are finished. These can be sown with quick maturing annuals including clarkia, godetia, cornflower, calendulas and viscarias.

As far as soil preparation is concerned, the majority of hardy and half hardy annuals do best in soil which is in good condition. It should not be too rich, for very generous feeding is likely to lead to lush growth and fewer flowers of poor substance. In other cases, growth may be so great that the plants become top heavy and the blooms easily damaged by wind and storm.

There are subjects suitable for dry, sunny places, for semi-shade, for stony ground, and for positions where the soil remains moist throughout the summer, so that no garden need be without some annuals. If the soil is in poor condition it will be helpful if a dressing of good compost or a mixture of granulated peat and hop manure can be forked into the top spit some weeks before sowing is done.

In addition, many gardeners find it an advantage to work in a good organic general fertiliser, say at the rate of 2 oz per square yard, although nothing which is of a forcing nature should be used. The addition of compost or peat is particularly useful on very light soil, improving its moisture holding capacity. Very heavy soil is rendered more porous and open.

Once compost and manure have been added, the ground should be given some time to settle down. Having forked through the surface and broken down the lumps, it is a good plan to lightly tread over the surface and make it uniformly firm. Puffy ground will lead to poor results, in that the plants are likely to suffer from lack of moisture during dry spells. After treading the surface evenly, it should be raked to a fine tilth.

Where complete borders are being sown with annuals, it is advisable to mark out the shapes of the patches before commencing to sow. If short pointed sticks are left in position this will avoid any overlapping in sowing. It is far better to sow in irregular shaped clumps than in lines, formal squares, or oblong blocks.

There are several methods of sowing annuals and probably the simplest of all is to scatter the seed thinly and as evenly as possible over the area in question. Then rake it in and press down the soil with the head of the rake. This, of course, does mean that there is a certain amount of wasting of seed, for some of the seedlings are bound to come up too thickly and thinning will have to be done.

If it is decided to sow in rows it is better to sow in small pinches at intervals in the drills, since it is necessary for each plant to have sufficient room to develop properly. Sowing as suggested will mean that only tiny patches will have to be thinned rather than the whole rows.

Distance between rows depends on the height of the plants as given on the seed packet. As a rough guide, allow a distance of half the height of the plants between the rows.

Depth of sowing is also important. Tiny seeds must not be buried deeply, or they will fail. On the other hand, very shallow sowing means that in the dry weather the seed may dry out. Sufficient moisture to help the seed germinate and encourage the seedlings to grow must always be available. Large seeds such as calendulas and nasturtiums should be covered to a depth equal to three times the diameter of the seed.

Seed is often sprinkled directly from the packet, doing so by a shaking motion to allow it to fall out. This can be a wasteful method leading to the necessity for much thinning out and loss of seedlings. A simpler method is to place the seed in the palm of one hand and to sow by taking pinches of seed with the finger and thumb of the other hand. As far as possible do not sow in windy weather for the seed can easily be blown away.

Although the flowers of some annuals last for only a short while and a few may shed their petals quickly after being cut, some species are quite long lasting as cut flowers. In fact the more the flowers are cut the more freely they produce fresh blooms. Certainly the majority of annuals are seen at their best in their growing positions but there are some which deserve consideration as cut blooms. A few, including nigella, *Gypsophila elegans* and *Saponaria vaccaria*, 'Pink Beauty', yield one crop and when grown on a commercial scale are often drawn up by the roots for sending to market.

The annual chrysanthemums are particularly long lasting, when cut, usually retaining their fresh appearance for ten to fourteen days. Of the single forms, 'Golden Glory' and 'Evening Star' are golden yellow, 'Eldorado' has a dark centre, while there are several excellent double yellow varieties. The Tricolor mixture takes in an attractive colour range.

Calendulas, particularly the Double Art Shades are great favourites for cutting, while the early flowering types of cosmos with their ferny foliage in warm colours including orange, are useful when a tall subject is needed. The double forms of Godetia last well, standing up to draughty conditions. Calliopsis, the annual coreopsis, is also a good lasting flower. Larkspurs, particularly if sown in the autumn hold their blooms, while the many forms of asters are dependable, especially if the water is changed frequently.

Sweet Peas in variety are always in demand. These remain fresh much longer if kept under fairly cool conditions. Sweet Sultan and zinnias are also excellent for cutting. The latter too, is especially valuable for late flowering.

The annual lupins are used for cutting and as a source of green manure. Usually the plants are dug into the ground before they come into flower, although some gardeners allow them to produce the central spike, which is cut, and the remainder of the plant dug in. This is a very valuable natural means of supplying nitrogen to the soil and increasing fertility.

Three

Annuals for the Greenhouse and Living Room

At one time glasshouses and conservatories were used to grow only exotic plants that required a considerable amount of heat to keep them healthy. With the great increase in the price of fuel and the lack of labour and time to maintain the larger structures, it became necessary to look for plants which would grow under cooler conditions. At the beginning of this century, annuals were rarely included in greenhouse or conservatory displays.

Because of necessity and the introduction of many more interesting annual species and varieties, they now play a large part in the glass-house display of both professional and amateur gardeners. In addition, the impressive displays of annuals at Chelsea and other national Flower Shows has increased the interest and revealed the wide range of plants which can be cultivated without difficulty.

It is not only the lesser known subjects which are so useful as greenhouse plants, but quite a number of items which we have for long grown in open ground have proved admirable grown under glass. These include such favourites as calendulas, clarkia, godetia, mignonette, and nasturtiums, which are dealt with in Chapter 8.

Sowing the seeds

While the usual seed trays allow a good quantity of seed to be sown, seed pans or pots may also be used. Where small amounts of individual items are being sown, they keep the soil more evenly moist. After putting the crocks or other drainage material at the bottom of the receptacles, the sowing medium is added. This can be the John Innes seed compost or something similar and should be made moderately firm, with the corners filled in. Sow the seed thinly—a help in this connection is to mix it with fine silver sand. Then cover with a light sprinkling of compost but never bury deeply.

In the case of very tiny seeds, these need merely be pressed into the compost and a little silver sand sprinkled over them. Having made sure the compost is nicely moist, which can be done by immersing the pots up to their rims in water and subsequently letting them drain, the receptacles should be placed in the greenhouse or frame, according to the subjects being grown. A steady temperature of about 60°F is ideal. Place a sheet of glass over the trays or pans and cover this with paper to exclude light. It is wise to lift the glass daily, so that the condensation can be wiped off. This will prevent the seeds and compost from becoming too moist in the places where drips would fall.

Once germination has occurred, the glass and paper are no longer required. Gradually accustom the seedlings to full light, and bring them near the glass, otherwise weak spindly growth will result. Water with great care, so that the moisture does not settle around the lower stems and roots, for this is one of the causes of damping off disease.

Pricking out seedlings

The term pricking out can be defined as the moving of very young seedlings while the root system is so small that it can be easily accommodated in a hole made by a little dibber about the size of a finger. This operation may be considered as an essential part in the production of good plants, and will ensure that all the greenhouse space available is taken up by really good specimens.

As soon as the seedlings begin to make progress, they need more room if they are to develop into shapely, sturdy specimens. Delay in moving them can sometimes result in a serious, if not permanent setback. They will also need more light, air, and food.

Sometimes, it is possible to move seedlings directly into individual pots at the first pricking out, but more often than not, they are best moved to other boxes or trays. Early moving will reduce the chances of damping off diseases occurring, although they should not attack if a good class compost is used and clean water is always applied with care.

If there is the slightest suggestion of disease or the plants fail to make even growth, the little stems should be closely examined at soil level. If there is a withering or blackening at that point, the affected plants should be removed and the remainder watered with a solution of Cheshunt Compound, which will normally prevent the disease spreading but will not cure it.

Although it is possible to prick seedlings out directly into soil blocks, this is not necessary with pot plants. As a space saver, the standard seed trays which are 2½ in deep, may be regarded as ideal. A simple, but good compost, should be used for the pricking off soil mixture, and the John Innes potting composts are suitable. Organic gardeners can make up a similar mixture, although they will leave out the artificial fertiliser and replace it with seaweed, fish or bone meal.

Make the compost reasonably firm in the boxes and use a little dibber which will make a hole big enough to take the roots of the seedlings without screwing them up. It should not be too sharply pointed, otherwise an air pocket may be left around the roots of the seedlings and lead to disappointing results. Do not shake off the soil adhering to the roots.

Where a lot of plants have regularly to be pricked out, it is worth securing a multi-dibber. These are like flat pieces of wood studded with metal or wooden knobs and spaced so that forty-eight holes are made over the surface of the standard size seed trays. This ensures an even spacing and uniform depth, which is another important point, for seedlings buried too deeply may easily damp off.

The exact time to prick out seedlings largely depends on the subjects being grown. In some cases it can be done within three or four days of germination, which will be before lateral roots have grown. The smaller the root system, the more easily the plants may be moved without injury and the less likelihood of a check. Experience shows that growth is definitely retarded if parts of the roots are broken.

In some cases it may be up to a fortnight before the seedlings are big enough to handle. This will mean there is a larger root system, so that an appropriate sized hole must be made when pricking out. Spacing the seedlings is also important.

If they are being moved individually to pots, the matter is simple, but if, first, they are transferred into other trays, they must be spaced according to their usual rate of growth and how long they are to remain in the trays. Overcrowded seedlings will become drawn and may suffer from malnutrition. There is also the problem of avoiding damage to the roots when the plants are finally moved to separate pots.

To give the seedlings every opportunity to do well, care is needed when filling the boxes or pots at the pricking out stage. Make the compost reasonably firm, and bring it to within a $\frac{1}{4}$ in of the top. The compost should also be nicely moist before attempting to extract the plants, but if it is too wet it will become a very messy job. Extraction will be easier if an end of the seed box is sharply tapped on a bench to shake the soil down and make a gap at the other end. The first seedlings can then be taken out easily.

A flat ended label is suitable for lifting out the plants with some soil adhering to the roots. Never grip the roots which easily become damaged thus opening the way for disease to attack. Make the holes large enough to take the roots without bending them.

Do not bury the seedlings deeply. They should be planted a little lower in the soil than the previous soil mark on the stems. Leave them standing upright and nicely firmed in the soil but avoid too much moving or touching of the stems after the plants have been inserted.

The proper watering of annuals growing in pots may well be considered one of the corner-stones of success. It is not always easy to determine when a plant should be given moisture. There is much to be said for the long used method of tapping the pot with the knuckles or a little wooden mallet. If the sound given out is hollow, one may assume that water is necessary; if the sound is dull and heavy, the soil is moist enough. These are not infallible signs but they are a definite indication as to the soil condition.

It is also necessary to decide the best means of supplying moisture, for even when the top soil is wet after the pots have been filled with water, one sometimes finds that the compost has not become uniformly moist.

Whilst there is nothing against watering from above so long as it is carefully done, it is best to stand pots which have holes in the bottom in shallow water, so that moisture works its way up through the compost. It is most unwise to leave most plants standing in saucers of water, for while too little moisture will lead to withering and the plants looking pale and sickly, too much water causes sourness of soil and decay of roots.

Waterlogging is fatal to all plants, for the air spaces which are in well drained compost, become filled with moisture and the roots are deprived of the oxygen they need. This leads to the destruction of the root hairs and then of the roots themselves.

Not only is moisture taken up by the roots, but it is lost through the surface soil and through the sides of the pots—that is, when the ordinary earthenware type is used. These are really better than glazed containers, which normally have no outlet to allow surplus water to escape.

Sometimes ordinary pots are placed in ornamental containers.

Arctotis Large Flowered hybrids

27

This is quite satisfactory so long as surplus water does not remain in the bottom of the bigger containers, for if it does sour and waterlogged compost leads to trouble. Perhaps the ideal way of growing many plants is to place them in an outer container and to pack sphagnum moss between the two containers, keeping it damp. Not only will dampness help to keep the foliage in good condition, but there is less likelihood of the compost drying out.

Pot plants should be watered only when they need it, for it is a mistake to water regularly every day or once a week. Some plants may need moisture at these intervals at certain times of the year, others will certainly not.

Watering therefore is a matter of using common sense and of applying it when necessary and not at specific times.

Potting on

If the pricking off operation is important, so is the subsequent moving of the plants to pots. There are two terms in general use for this job, one is potting up or potting off, which is used for when the seedlings are moved from the seed tray or pan into their first pots. The second term is potting on, and indicates the moving of a plant from a small pot to a larger size.

Apart from the question of space, the main reason why young plants are not moved into the pots they will eventually occupy, is that too much root room in the early stages of growth is inclined to cause the plants to produce an abundance of stem and leaf growth at the expense of the flowers.

Potting back is a term not often used, but it indicates the reducing of the size of the ball of soil and roots and putting it into a smaller pot. Re-potting of course is merely the shaking out of the soil from the ball of roots and putting the plant back in the same pot, but using a fresh soil mixture.

Whenever plants are moved to fresh pots, the ball of soil should be made nicely moist before the job begins. Particularly during the late autumn and winter months, the fresh compost used should be brought indoors for a time, so that it is more or less of the same temperature as the greenhouse. This avoids the possibility of a check from the soil being cold and wet.

Firm potting is important but this does not mean ramming down

28

the soil. If this is done, the young fibrous roots may be damaged or even broken. Once in pots, the plants should be given a good watering to ensure the roots are in close contact with the soil. Always use clean pots. It is possible to procure special pot brushes which fit the inside of the pot. These are most useful where a number of pots are being cleaned and washed.

Good drainage is most essential and each pot should have a suitable piece of crock or broken pot placed over the drainage hole, concave side downwards. Several small pieces can be added, although plants which will be potted on will need less than those which have reached their final pots. These crocks can be covered with a layer of coarse leaf mould before the compost is put in.

There are many kinds of pots on the market, some of which are quite ornamental. The long-used earthenware types remain very serviceable and are among the best for general purposes. These can, of course, be placed in ornamental vases if desired when the plants are brought into the living room.

Earthenware pots are available in many sizes and they are often referred to in numbers, such as 60s, or 48s. These figures refer to the number of pots in a cast—the way in which the pots are sold by the manufacturers—so that the 48 size pot simply means that there are 48 to the cast. Unless one knows the exact size, this is not very helpful.

The following table gives the number of pots to the cast:

Descriptive name	Diameter	Depth
Thimbles	2 in	2 in
Thumbs	$2\frac{1}{2}$ in	$2\frac{1}{2}$ in
Small sixties	$2\frac{3}{4}$ in	$3\frac{1}{4}$ in
Large sixties	$3\frac{1}{2}$ in	$3\frac{1}{2}$ in
Fiftyfours	$4\frac{1}{2}$ in	5 in
Fortyeights	5 in	5 in
Thirtytwos	6 in	6 in
Twentyfours	$8\frac{1}{2}$ in	8 in
Sixteens	$9\frac{1}{2}$ in	9 in
Twelves	11 in	10 in
Eights	12 in	11 in
Sixes	13 in	12 in
Fours	15 in	13 in
Twos	18 in	14 in

This table is particularly useful for the person who wishes to obtain only a few pots. He can be sure of the size, for the name indicates both the top diameter and depth of the pots.

In addition, there are pots known as Long Toms, which are similar to the 60 size pots, but deeper. Orchid pots are provided with holes around the sides as well as in the bottom. Seed pans, which are as wide but not very deep, are made in several sizes and often used in preference to seed trays.

Many subjects which grow in the greenhouse, frame or living room are sometimes inclined to become tall and thin. To minimise this possibility, the plants should be grown fairly near the glass. It is only in a comparatively few cases that a single stem is required and it is therefore wise to take out the growing points of any seedlings which do not show signs of making side shoots.

Nip out the top growth to just above a joint. This will result in the production of laterals leading to sturdy, shapely plants. One of the difficulties in raising various plants from seed is that we are inclined to grow more plants of individual items than we have room to accommodate. It is very easy to sow a whole box of seedlings but such quantities do take up a lot of room. A batch of say 3 dozen $2\frac{1}{2}$ in pots will need a space of $3\frac{1}{2}$sq ft, while a dozen 5 in pots takes up 6sq ft.

Feeding

A plant growing in a pot has a greatly restricted root run and the roots cannot search widely for nourishment and moisture. Unless reserve quantities of manures have been incorporated in the potting compost, and this is by no means wise, liquid feeding becomes essential. Although certain plants may require particular types of food, those growing in pots will almost without exception greatly benefit from a good organic liquid fertiliser. As in so many ways when growing plants, it is possible to be 'over kind' when supplying nourishment.

No type of feeding should be given immediately after plants have been pricked out or moved to bigger pots, for then they require time to settle down. It is, however, helpful if feed is given a week or so before potting on is done. Never apply fertilisers when the compost is dry and make sure the main feeding is done when the plants are in full growth. They do not need it when they are dormant, or approaching their resting period.

Any kind of feeding, liquid or otherwise, should be carefully considered before application, for anything used which is very rich in nitrogen, is liable to lead to abundant leaf growth but may delay flowering. More nitrogen should be applied when increased vegetative growth is required.

For flower production and the formation of a good root system, both potash and phosphates are needed. These properties can all be found in animal or other organic manures and experience has proved they are more effective when applied in liquid form, than mixed dry with the compost. This does not imply that top dressings are ineffective. Sometimes they are very useful and, watered in gradually, they release their feeding material over a long period. Even so, liquid food judiciously applied, is best. Given too strong, or too frequently, it can lead to bud drop.

Where normal manure and soot water cannot be secured or made up, one may with safety rely on the seaweed fertilisers such as Maxicrop or Neptune's Bounty, while Liquinure and Sangral are both good. All must be used in accordance with the directions on the containers.

It must not be thought that feeding at twice the strength recommended, will give results which are twice as good. Far from it, such action may lead to all sorts of troubles. Little and often should be the rule with liquid feeding. If it is started when the plants are young and have made a good root system, entirely satisfactory, free-flowering plants will be built up.

Four

Annuals as Cut Flowers

While the main reason for growing annuals is to provide colour in the garden in the shortest possible time, they are often grown as a means of obtaining a supply of cut flowers for indoor decoration. There must be few homes where flowers are not used. With the increased interest in flower arrangement, and the fact that as with most commodities, shop prices are rising, many more people are becoming interested in growing their own blooms.

In addition, there are many first class subjects which are never seen in florist's shops since they do not market well, but if cut straight from the garden they are most attractive in living rooms.

To overcome the objection that the cutting of blooms spoils the garden display, especially where the demand is heavy, it is usually possible to grow the plants in a separate plot. In fair sized gardens, space is often allowed in the vegetable plot for a cut flower bed. This prevents denuding an ornamental area. In such cases the plants may be grown in rows for ease of cutting instead of in irregular beds used in the flower garden.

With thought, proper arrangement, and the right selection of plants, it is possible to provide cut flowers from annuals for the greater part of the year. This means that some species and varieties will be sown in the autumn so that they bloom early, and before plants raised from seed sown under glass early in the year, or in the open ground from April onwards.

While it is not possible to mention all the annuals which are suitable for cutting, the following selection will give an idea of the range available.

Ageratum is normally used as an edging plant, but the species *A. mexicanum*, grows 15–18 in tall, the soft lavender-blue flowers looking well when cut. Sow under glass in the early spring and put the plants outdoors in late May.

Asters have for long been greatly valued as cut flowers. The older strains of Ostrich Feather and the Victoria type have been greatly improved. Besides this, many new types and strains have been introduced, a notable advance being the advent of the wilt and rust-resistant varieties.

The newer Ostrich Plume sorts in separate colours are early flowering, with large loose feathery heads on 15–18 in stems. These are followed by the Californian Giant mixed with strong stems up to 2 ft high. The Perfection mixed has large full centred flowers, while the wilt-resistant Powderpuff strain has rounded heads. Even taller growing, are the Giant Comet Asters which have most elegant blooms.

The Giant Princess mixed asters are wilt-resistant, their mid-season blooms having a cushion-like centre. The Duchess asters are of fairly recent introduction, the huge incurved blooms being carried on stiff 2 ft stems. Cut young they are very long lasting. Colours include crimson, blue, rose, white and yellow.

Single asters are always useful for cutting and the 'Southcote Beauty' strain is particularly graceful. The *Super Chinensis* mixed are a real advance. The large flowers have two or more rows of long petals on rigid stems. The slender quilled petals of the *Rayonante* asters makes them outstanding, as in the Unicum type.

All can be grown under the half hardy treatment or sown directly in the open ground in early May.

Agrostemma githago is the Corn Cockle, the variety specially good for cutting being 'Milas', which has pale rosy-lilac flowers on 2½–3 ft stems. It is free blooming, the long stiff stems being graceful, making it a fine subject for garden decoration and for cutting from May until September.

Amaranthus caudatus is better known as Love-lies-bleeding, the seed of which can be grown outdoors in April. The long, drooping tassels are amaranth-red, while there is a greenish-white form. Treated well, the tassels last a long time. Plants may also be cultivated in pots.

Calendula is one of the hardiest and most serviceable of all annuals, and it can, given reasonable conditions, often be found in bloom throughout the year. Its one fault is its tendency to seed freely, so that it is essential to remove unwanted seedlings before they smother other nearby plants.

Although calendulas *will* grow almost anywhere and seed simply sprinkled on the ground and roughly worked in, will produce quite good results, for the finest flowers a sunny position and a fairly well drained soil should be chosen. Seed sown in September will produce blooms from March onwards, especially if cloches are used during the winter, while sowings made in the early spring will provide blooms from late July onwards.

There are a number of good varieties in many shades of yellow and orange, ranging in height from 15 in to 2 ft. Among the best are 'Campfire', deep orange; 'Chrysantha', canary-yellow; 'Indian Maid', light orange, dark centre; 'Orange King', rich orange and 'Radio', bright orange quilled petals.

Centaurea cyanus, better known as Cornflower, needs no description. Plants can be raised from seed sown in September for producing flowers in March and April or, sown in the spring, they will flower from June onwards. They are best sown where they are to flower, although carefully done the seedlings can be transplanted. Apart from the tall growing sorts of which the double flowers are either blue, mauve, rose or white, all about 3 ft high, there are various sorts growing a foot high, which are quite suitable for cutting. These include: 'Jubilee Gem', blue; 'Lilac Lady', and 'Rose Gem', carmine-rose.

C. moschata is the Sweet Sultan, which if cut when young will last at least a week. The sweetly scented, fluffy, thistle-like heads, grow on stems 18 in high, although there is a taller strain having very large flowers. The colours are shades of purple, mauve, yellow and white.

The Annual Chrysanthemums are particularly long lasting when cut, usually retaining their fresh appearance for 10–14 days. Of the single forms, 'Golden Glory' and 'Evening Star' are golden yellow, 'Eldorado' has a dark centre, while there are several excellent double-yellow varieties. The tricolor mixture takes in an attractive colour range.

Clarkia is a favourite annual of easy culture. It thrives in the sun and while preferring a light soil, will grow well in heavier ground.

It will not transplant well, so seed should be sown thinly. In addition to their value as plants for the garden, and for cutting for house decoration, clarkias grow well in pots, and if sown in pots in the autumn, they will flower in the cool greenhouse in the early spring.

Growing 18–24 in high, they are available in named sorts, among the best being the following varieties of *C. elegans:* 'Albatross', white; 'Chieftain', mauve; 'Enchantress', salmon-pink; 'Lady Satin Rose', rosy-carmine; 'Orange King', orange-scarlet; 'Salmon Bouquet' and 'Vesuvius', reddish-orange.

Coreopsis. Apart from the well-known perennial coreopsis, there are some excellent annual varieties which are sometimes catalogued as calliopsis. Seed can be sown directly into flowering quarters, or plants may be raised under glass. They transplant well, and flower from July onwards, varying in height from 9–10 in to 2½ ft.

C. drummondi 'Golden Crown' is yellow with a dark centre, while there are many good varieties of *C. tinctoria* including: 'Crimson King'; 'Dazzler', maroon-crimson with yellow edge to petals; 'Fire King', scarlet; 'Golden Sovereign', gold-yellow and 'The Garnet', crimson-scarlet.

Cosmos or Cosmea. These plants are of value both for their flowers and feathery foliage. The usual plan is to sow seeds under glass in March, pricking off the seedlings in the usual way, and then to plant outdoors in light soil during April or May. Recently it has become a common practice to sow seeds directly into open ground from mid-April onwards. The tall growing species *C. bipinnatus* grows up to 4 ft high, having pink, crimson or white flowers. A form known as 'Sensation' is reliable and available in shades of pink, some having a crimson centre. There is a crested centred form, and several varieties with a yellow or orange shading.

Dimorphotheca. Star of the Veldt. These gaily coloured daisy-like flowers are superb for using alone or with other subjects. Like arctotis, they need a sunny place preferring light ground slightly on the dry side. In dull weather the flowers remain partially closed as they do at night. Seed can be sown under glass early in April, but best results come by sowing in May where the plants are to bloom. They usually show colour about 2 months after sowing. Height varies from 12–18 in.

The *D. aurantiaca* hybrids take in such colours as apricot, buff, biscuit, yellow, lemon, orange, and white, some having a dark centre.

Emilia, better known as Cacalia or Tassel Flower, is a charming subject not usually reckoned among cut flower subjects, but for miniature arrangements and posies it is ideal. Its freely produced, clustered flower heads of bright scarlet which show from June to October, are carried on stems of a foot or more.

Eschscholtzia. While often used in bunches of mixed flowers, this subject loses its petals too quickly to be of great value for cutting. In a sunny situation and a rather light, dry soil, the plants will flower very freely from June onwards. The finely divided grey-green foliage can be cut with the flowers which are available in very many colour tones, including cream, yellow, orange, rose, carmine, crimson-scarlet and golden bronze.

Gaillardia. The annual varieties can either be sown under glass and transplanted later, or into their flowering quarters. They bloom from July onwards and grow 15–18 in high. There are a number of good varieties of *G. pulchella*, including: picta, crimson tipped yellow; *lorenziana*, double mixed with globular flower heads; and 'Indian Chief', bronze-red; also some single forms.

Gaura lindheimeri, while not a striking plant, is useful for cutting. Its long, graceful sprays of white flowers appear from July to October, Growing 3 ft or so high, it thrives in any good garden position.

Godetia is another popular annual of easy culture. It is handsome when growing in the garden and when cut, thriving in any ordinary, well drained soil. Thin out the seedlings early, to encourage bushy growth.

Seeds are best sown where they are to flower during March or April, although they may also be sown in September. There are both dwarf and tall strains, the former (9–12 in high) also looking well when grown in pots. Well grown plants of the tall type will reach 2½–3 ft.

Gypsophila elegans is a much used annual of which seed may be sown in the open, either in September or in succession during the spring. Almost any soil is suitable, chalky being particularly good.

The upright, branching plants grow 18 in high and, in the case of the 'Covent Garden' strain, the flowers are fairly large and pure white. There are forms having rose or crimson flowers, all varieties being suitable for using in mixed bunches or arrangements.

Helianthus. A number of forms of the annual Sunflower are excellent for indoor use. All grow in good garden soil and may be sown in the spring, where they are to flower. Some of the best are to be had in shades of yellow, purplish-red, orange with dark centres and red tipped yellow. All flower from July onwards.

Lavatera trimestris should be sown in the early spring, where they are to bloom. Space the plants well and they will develop into bushy specimens, the 2–3 ft stems carrying many semi-trumpet shaped flowers. *L. splendens* is pink. There is both a rose and a white form but it is the variety Loveliness or Sunset, with its rose-pink blooms, which is outstanding.

Leptosyne stillmanni is a hardy annual which can be sown where it is to bloom, during April and May. The lemon-yellow, daisy-like flowers are attractive, as is the double form, 'Golden Rosette'.

Linaria. Rather like miniature antirrhinums, the linarias or Toadflax are continuous flowering subjects. Easy to grow, they prefer a sunny position and a fairly light soil. Sow in March or April, where the plants are to bloom. Flowers appear in quick succession from early June until October. Valuable for the smaller arrangements and posies, there are a number of excellent species.

L. cymbalaria, the Kenilworth Ivy, produces attractive trailing growths which can be used to advantage in many types of floral creations; the flowers are lilac, rose or white, most having a yellow throat mark. *L. maroccana* is violet-purple marked with yellow, producing its pretty little flowers in many colours on spikes of 10–15 in. The 'Fairy Bouquet' Mixture grows only 9 in high.

Linum is another easy to grow plant, which can be sown in succession. While the ordinary pale blue variety has its uses, it is the scarlet Flax *L. grandiflorum rubrum*, which is useful to flower arrangers. Growing 12–18 in high, the erect branching stems bear a profusion of blooms throughout the summer and early autumn.

Malope flowers freely and continuously from July to October. *M. grandiflora* has rose-red flowers, while there are pink and white forms all growing 2–3 ft high.

Marigold is a half-hardy plant of simple culture which may be grown in the same way as asters. There are, nowadays, several strains containing colours ranging from red, orange to yellow, which grow more than 3 ft high, and produce really large, round flowers. No doubt the size and weight of the latter is a cause of their sometimes having weak heads, although the best modern sorts have quite tough stems.

Recently some varieties with non-scented foliage have been introduced and if these prove to be reliable, the African and dwarf French varieties too, will undoubtedly be much more used for cutting purposes.

Matricaria. A number of interesting plants belong to this family, some being better known as chrysanthemum species. *M. capensis* is really a perennial, but is worth growing as an annual. Sow seed in March under glass and put the plants outdoors in May. It forms a bushy plant of 2 ft in height, has heads of white flowers, the double form lasting better than the single. The foliage is 'chrysanthemum scented'. *M. inodora* has from June to October single white flowers on 12–15 in stems and is useful for all floral work. It can be sown in April in its flowering position.

Coleus Master Blends

Mignonette. Much valued because of its fragrance, this is not a difficult plant to grow. It prefers soil in which there is lime and a well prepared firm site. It can be sown outdoors from April onwards, or under glass. A sowing made in September in pots will provide early spring growing plants. Early thinning out is advisable for it is stocky, bushy plants which will produce the most blooms. The Latin name of this subject is *Reseda odorata*. There are a number of varieties growing a foot or more in height. They include: 'Bismarck', large spikes of bright red; 'Golden Goliath', yellow; 'Machet Improved', red; and 'Red Monarch', bright red.

Chrysanthemum tricolor mixed

Molucella, often known as Bells of Ireland, and the Shell Flower is best sown under glass in March or early April, and planted outdoors towards the end of May. It is sometimes slow to germinate and growers have found it of advantage to sow the seed early in the year in a just moist, sandy compost and then to cover the pots or boxes with glass and stand outdoors in a sheltered place. If subsequently they are brought into a greenhouse temperature of 65°F, the seeds germinate well. *M. laevis* produces spikes of large pale green calyces which make it so attractive as a foil for other flowers. It lasts several weeks in water and may be dried and used in autumn designs.

Nasturtiums, although often regarded as 'common', are most useful for indoor decoration. The colour range is exceedingly wide and both the shape and size of the leaves enables them to fit in to all sorts of designs. They are of the easiest culture. All that needs to be done is to cover the seed with a $\frac{1}{2}$ in or so of soil and germination will occur in a short while. They do well in poor and even dry soil and will often go on blooming until the early winter.

The newer dwarf double mixed strain is remarkable for its colour range, many of the flowers being scented. 'Empress of India' has very dark foliage and crimson-red flowers, while 'Ryburgh Gem' has variegated leaves. The long trails of the climbing nasturtium have many uses. In the garden these growths must be restricted so that the plants do not exceed their allotted space. Used alone, or with other subjects, here is a flower which is of the utmost value.

Nemesia. Although chiefly used as an edging plant, *N. strumosa suttonii* will grow 12–15 in high, making it an excellent cut flower. Although usually grown as a mixture, there are separate colours available including shades of blue, pink, red and orange. Sow under glass in early spring and move to the open ground in May.

Nemophila insignis although only 6–8 in high is charming in miniature decorations and posies. The clear sky-blue flowers have white centres. It should be sown where it is to bloom either in the spring or September and according to when it is sown, flowers are available from May onwards.

Nigella, better known as Love-in-a-Mist, is another subject of the easiest culture. Sow where the plants are to bloom either in the spring or September. The flowers on 12–18 in stems, often higher, have light green, feathery foliage surrounding the petals.

The best known variety of *N. damascena* is 'Miss Jekyll', cornflower blue and there is a white form, while 'Persian Jewels' takes in a range of colours such as rose, pink, carmine, and lavender. The seed pods dry well and can be used for winter decoration.

Phlox drummondii are rather too straggly for general use as a cut flower, but they have a limited value where slender stems are required in a more or less drooping or hanging position. Seed is sown under glass in spring, the plants being put in the open in early May. There are many bright colours, some with blotched petals.

Rudbeckia is another annual which is easy to grow and valuable for cutting from the end of July onwards. The species *R. bicolor* has yellow petals with a dark central cone, but it is its varieties which are particularly showy. These include: 'Kelvedon Star', 18–24 in high, the golden-yellow petals having a mahogany zone at the base, as well as a brown cone centre; *R. hirta*, is often known as Black-Eyed Susan and the hybrids take in many shades of yellow, orange and bronze-red. Sow in early spring under glass and transplant in April or May to flowering positions.

Salpiglossis is a half-hardy annual raised in warmth in the early spring. It flourishes outdoors in well drained soil and unexposed positions. Growing 1½–2½ ft high, it produces from July to September funnel-shaped flowers in bright colours, including crimson, scarlet, yellow and blue with prominent richly coloured veins.

Saponaria is used for mixing with cut flowers in the same way as the annual gypsophila. *Saponaria vaccaria* is of the simplest culture. Sown in open ground in early spring or September, it produces sprays of flowers from April onwards according to when sown. The variety rosea has large, pink flowers, but the best one is 'Pink Beauty' growing 2–3 ft high.

Scabious. Sweet Scabious is often known as the Pin Cushion Flower, which gives an idea of the appearance of the blooms. There is a tremendously wide colour range, including: blue, crimson, coral-pink, rosy-crimson, yellow and maroon-black, all having wide petals with a pin cushion-like centre and they are varieties of *S. atropurpurea*. They like a sunny, well drained position and grow 2½ ft high, with firm, straight stems. Early sowings should be made under glass and these can be succeeded by outdoor sowings from mid-May.

Senecio is a large varied family among which is *S. elegans*, usually offered in catalogues as Jacobaea elegans. Often treated as half-hardy annuals, they can be sown where they are to flower outdoors in April, in ordinary soil and a sunny position. Usually available in mixtures, the colours include crimson, mauve, purple, rose and white, the double flowers looking like little pompoms on 18–24 in stems.

Sweet Sultan. See Centaurea.

Stocks. Provided the right varieties are selected, these are excellent flowers for cutting. While sometimes used, the Ten Week strains have a tendency to wilt if not plunged in water at once, especially if cut under dry conditions. The Hansen strain is particularly good. Not only is it possible to concentrate on plants producing double flowers, since these can be selected in the seedling stage by the colour of the foliage, but the stems are strong. The older Ten Week are still reliable, but where extra large spikes are required the 'Giant Excelsior Column' growing up to 2½ ft are really magnificent.

Stocks like a well prepared site with humus material worked into the soil well before planting time. Cut the blooms before they are fully developed, and strip off the lower leaves before arranging the stems, which will otherwise become very messy and may spoil the blooms. The colour range is wide, taking in pink, lavender, mauve, red, yellow and white.

Sweet Peas are invaluable for cutting and provided they are grown in well prepared enriched soil produce an abundance of flowers. For the earliest blooms sow in the cold frame or under cloches in early October and, for flowering from June onwards, in gentle heat in January or February. Varieties are a matter of choice, and the colour range is extremely wide as will be seen on reference to the catalogues of specialist growers.

Tithonia, if treated as a half-hardy annual is a splendid subject for cutting. Sow under glass and transfer out of doors at the end of May.

Tripteris is a fairly uncommon annual now officially grouped as Osteospermum. Sow under glass in March or in the open during April and May. A sunny place should be chosen for the plants and an ordinary, good, well drained soil. In dull weather and in the evening the flowers partially close which is a drawback. *T. hyoseroides* has large, orange-yellow flowers on 2 ft stems.

Venidium. The Namaqualand Daisy is best treated as a half-hardy annual and sown in heat, although it is possible to sow seed in open ground from late April onwards. *V. fastuosum* produces flowers from early June onwards, often 4 in or more in diameter. The brilliant orange flowers have a purplish zone in the centre.

Zinnias, of which many strains have been introduced during recent years, all require similar treatment. Sow in early March in a temperature of 60°F and prick out the seedlings 2 in apart when big enough to handle, or better still, put straight into small pots. They are hardened off for planting outdoors in early June. Allow at least 15 in between the plants and as they develop, feed with liquid manure.

Sowing in Autumn

Sowing and the general culture of annuals for cutting is the same as that for garden decoration. There are, however, different requirements for autumn sowings, while the range of subjects for this purpose is, of course, rather limited. Ideally, the site for autumn sowings should be one manured for a previous crop. Avoid using quick acting fertilisers, which usually lead to rapid growth with poor quality blooms.

The humus condition should be good and it will be helpful to work in hoof and horn, or bone meal, which will provide feeding matter for the spring and summer. Under mild conditions, sowing can be delayed until the third week in September, while in some seasons, it is quite satisfactory to make sowings right at the end of that month. Autumn sowings must be concentrated on subjects which will stand varying conditions, although if cloches are available, they may be used to cover the plants at intervals.

Even when fairly clean land is used, annual and perennial weeds may soon become a nuisance. This is why it is advisable to prepare the ground well in advance of sowing, since then it will not only have time to settle, but weed seeds will germinate and can be dealt with before flowers are sown.

Cornflowers are always in demand, especially the blue varieties. Drill the rows 1½ ft apart, with a wider pathway after every 3 or 4 rows to allow for picking.

Calendulas such as 'Orange King' also do well from an autumn sowing and these should be drilled a foot apart. Thin out the seedlings so they finally stand 9 in apart.

Candytuft, clarkia and godetia can all be sown in rows 9 in apart, allowing 6 in between the plants. These provide an abundance of early blooms.

Gypsophila elegans white, and the pink form, as well as *Saponaria vaccaria* and Viscaria mixed are other good standbys. Sow them in rows 8–10 in apart.

Larkspurs are particularly good for autumn sowing, although for these, the middle of August is about the right time, so that stout plants develop before winter. Make the drills 18 in apart, and thin the seedlings to 12 in. Most plants grow 3 or 4 ft high, and flower from early July. Always cut the spikes before the flowers are fully open.

Nigella 'Miss Jekyll', is another good subject for autumn sowing, flowering from the end of May onwards. Make the drills a foot apart and sow thinly, for the seedlings do not transplant easily.

Five

Annuals for Exhibition

Flower shows, particularly in villages, have been held in Britain for centuries. Their existence is largely due to the interest and devotion of gardeners from all walks of life. To-day, there are annual shows held in an increasing number of towns and villages, ranging from small displays in a tent or hall, to the more pretentious exhibitions at Chelsea and Southport.

Although show schedules cater for so many classes, those for annuals are the easiest to fill since they can be produced in the shortest time and without any complicated cultural requirements. Almost all who will exhibit are more concerned with the honour of winning rather than any monetary gains.

Apart from the actual growing of the plants, the most important point about showing annuals is to meet the rules of the show schedule. However meritorious an exhibit may be, if it does not meet requirements demanded, it cannot win.

Matters to specially observe include, first that the exhibit in an annual class is really an annual. For instance, it will not do to enter an antirrhinum since this subject is a perennial, although frequently grown as an annual. Then if the schedule asks for six stems, it is inviting disqualification to enter a larger or smaller number. In a class for separate colours a mixture would not be acceptable. Take note too, so that half-hardy annuals are not included if the schedule asks for hardy annuals and vice versa.

If a class calls for three vases of annuals in three distinct kinds the exhibitor could use say—calendulas, nigella and viscaria, but not three different varieties of any one or of any other annual.

In this and all other matters concerning a show entry, it is important to study the schedule well in advance of show day, so that exhibits can be properly entered. Whatever the schedule requires must be obeyed for the judge has to carry out the instructions the show committee makes regarding exhibits.

Not to conform makes it very probable that an exhibit will be disqualified, however good the flowers may be.

Attention too must be given to the use of vases. Some societies provide vases, while others allow competitors to use their own. Where this is so, avoid those which are of gaudy appearance, so that attention is directed to the exhibit and not the vase. Make sure too, if the schedule says that a bowl as opposed to a vase is to be used, that this is done—if not disqualification will be the result.

Select vases in keeping with the flowers being shown. Do not use flowers with long stems in squat vases, or blooms with short stems in vases which are tall and narrow necked.

While many exhibitors find it satisfactory to cut annuals on the morning of the show, it is, wherever possible, best to gather them the previous evening, but not when the stems are limp because the sun has been shining on them for some hours. After carefully cutting the stems, place them immediately in deep containers of water without, of course, wetting the actual blooms.

This will lead to the stems becoming quite turgid and will keep the flowers in good condition for a long time.

Many annuals can be sown in the autumn. This means they gain an early start with strong growth and usually earlier flowering with better formed blooms. There is always the possibility that during a very severe winter the plants may be spoiled or entirely destroyed, but the risk is well worth while. Autumn sown plants make it possible to enter the early shows, while sowings early in the year will provide blooms for the summer and autumn exhibitions.

Many annuals are judged on a points system, which can be of great importance when there is fierce competition. As a guide the following is the way in which certain annuals are judged. Information comes from the *Horticultural Show Hand-book* by permission of the Royal Horticultural Society.

Larkspur. Condition 6 points. Spikes 6 points. Colour 5 points. Uniformity 3 points.—Total 20 points.

African Marigolds. Condition 4 points. Form of flower 5 points. Colour 4 points. Stems 3 points. Uniformity 4 points.—Total 20 points.

Stocks. Condition 4 points. Spike 6 points. Form of flower 3 points. Colour 4 points. Uniformity 3 points.—Total 20 points.

Sweet Peas. Trueness of colour and freshness of bloom 7 points. Placement of bloom 4 points. Size and form of bloom 6 points. Stem proportionate to size of bloom 3 points.—Total 20 points.

Zinnias. Condition 4 points. Form of flower 4 points. Colour 4 points. Stems 5 points. Uniformity 3 points.—Total 20 points.

There is usually more rivalry in the sweet pea class than in most of the other annuals, which means that competition is severe. This is why it is customary for sweet pea growers to cultivate their plants on the cordon system. This means rather more effort in cultivation than when the plants are grown simply for decoration.

The plants are not allowed to grow in their natural manner, but are restricted to one or sometimes two main stems. All of the other growths and side shoots, as well as tendrils, are removed before they develop. This means that the remaining leaves will grow large and the flowers be much stronger than if growth is unrestricted. Each plant will need a separate support and it is usually necessary to have extra supports at the end of each row, with wires or strings running between the end supports. Extra feeding can be given as the plants develop but not until they have produced a number of flowers. Nothing of a forcing nature should be used since the aim should be to produce stocky growth with petals of firm texture.

The stems should be cut as near to the axil as possible to ensure a good length of stem and as far as possible no spikes with less than 4 florets should be included. Do not cut the spikes with all the florets fully opened: the uppermost ones should be half-open. Place the spikes in water immediately after cutting keeping them in a cool, light, airy place, making sure to keep the blooms dry. A short while in water will improve the sweet peas, helping the petals to fill out and acquire a fresh clean appearance.

The spikes are arranged so that the base appears to be slightly fan-shaped, all blooms facing roughly toward the front and the spikes fairly close, but so that the florets do not overlap. The longest stems are kept to the centre and back, the shortest in front. The usual method is to insert 5 or 6 spikes at the back of the vase leaning slightly backwards. The remaining blooms are then filled in to the front of the vase with the very best spikes well in evidence. All spikes should consist of evenly spaced florets with no gaps, for the latter is an indication of improper cultivation. Sweet Pea foliage is all that is necessary excepting in the decorative classes where other types of foliage may be used, notably *Asparagus plumosus* or *A. sprengeri*. Even these cannot be used if the schedule specifically states that the flowers *and* foliage used must be from annual plants.

This is also an important matter where entries for other flowers are exhibited. If the schedule calls for a vase or bowl of annuals with foliage make sure the foliage used comes from an annual subject otherwise the exhibit will be disqualified.

There are, of course, quite a lot of annuals which will provide suitable foliage. These include many of the attractive annual grasses such as *Briza gracilis*, *Coix lacryma-jobi*, *Hordeum jubatum* and *Lagurus ovatus*. The leaves of the ornamental *Zea japonica* (maize) are also useful. Other suitable foliage subjects are perilla, kochia, amaranthus, and artemesia. You could also use the young foliage of *Gypsophila elegans*, but not of the perennial *G. paniculata* and its varieties.

Many show schedules cater for annuals grown in pots. There is a very wide range of subjects suitable for this purpose. The majority of these are grown in the greenhouse and general culture is dealt with in the chapter on annuals for the greenhouse.

Perhaps the first test is to choose subjects which can be brought into best condition by show day. It is always advisable to cultivate a few more plants than will be needed for the class, which sometimes is for a single specimen or, on other occasions, three or six plants are required.

The range is wide and attractive. Subjects worth considering include: *Anchusa capensis*, browallia, calendulas, cuphea, *Celosia plumosa*, mignonette, nemesia, schizanthus, stocks and zinnias.

Care of Plants

The majority of annuals grown in pots for exhibition purposes will be raised and kept under glass. Because of this, ventilation must be freely provided to encourage sturdy growth of good colour. Ideally, temperatures should vary with light intensity, being lower as light intensity falls, and higher as it increases. A very high temperature when light intensity is low leads to an unbalanced growth, liable to disease.

The watering of exhibition plants calls for regular attention. Development depends on water, which is necessary for all activities of the plant, not the least for the transportation of mineral substances from the roots to the foliage, and every other part of the plant.

Over-watering must be avoided, since it easily leads to sourness of soil. The use of drainage material in the form of broken crocks placed on the bottom of the pots should minimise this possibility. Even so, never allow plants to wilt for want of moisture. Although slight wilting may do little permanent harm, if plants are badly affected, their development may be seriously, perhaps permanently retarded.

Always give the compost a good soaking, for sprinklings do little good. Often they cause harm by bringing roots too near the surface. As far as possible, water early in the day so that the foliage is dry at nightfall, making it less susceptible to harm from sudden drops in temperature. In hot weather it is often necessary to water more than once daily.

Never allow annuals to remain in pots where there is little root room. Common sense will dictate when plants should be potted on or moved to bigger pots. It is, however, a mistake to provide very large pots unless the plants are vigorous growing. Large pots of soil where there are few roots soon become sour, leading to all kinds of disorders. Provide shade according to need, remembering that too much sun can lessen the depth of colour and lower the value of the exhibit.

There are various ways of staging an exhibition of pot plants. In many cases the Show organisers provide staging, sometimes in tiers; in others the placing of the pots is left to the exhibitor. Occasionally one is able to plunge the pots in peat on the staging, which is a great help where the Show is of several days duration, since the moist peat keeps the compost from drying out.

The question of whether the pots can be placed in ornamental containers will be decided by the wording of the schedule. If it is allowed, some consideration should be given to the colours used, since anything blatant or gaudy would almost certainly detract from the plants themselves and might also distract the attention of the judges.

If you stand some of your pots on pedestals or blocks to give height, make sure they are placed firmly so they do not over-balance. It is best to avoid a group exhibit having sloping corners. Make certain that fading blooms and discoloured foliage are removed without damaging the plants, or spoiling their shape, while any necessary supports should be inconspicuous.

Whilst varieties are largely a matter of personal choice, there are many which are first class for show purposes. Among these are the following, of which there are numerous forms.

Asters	Gypsophila	Phlox
Calendula	Helichrysum	Salpiglossis
Calliopsis	Larkspur	Saponaria
Candytuft	Marigold	Statice
Centaurea	Mignonette	Sweet Sultan
Celosia	Molucella	Stocks
Clarkia	Nemesia	Ursinia
Cosmos	Nigella	Viscaria
Dimorphotheca	Phacelia	Zinnia

Hibiscus trionum

Reference to the catalogues of specialist seedsmen will disclose how wide is the range of named varieties, and in many cases these same catalogues give advice regarding exhibiting annuals.

Sweet Peas are a particular example of a subject of which there are many varieties most suitable for exhibition purposes. New sorts are introduced annually, so that no list can remain quite up to date, but the following varieties are very reliable for the show bench and will undoubtedly continue to remain so for some years.

Hollyhock Double Annual mixed

'Leamington', lavender; 'Noel Sutton', mid-blue; 'Ballerina', cream with rose picotee edge; 'Princess Elizabeth', salmon-pink; 'Hunters Moon', deep cream; 'White Ensign'; 'Geranium Pink Improved', rose suffused salmon-orange; 'Percy Izzard', cherry-red; 'Carlotta', rosy-carmine; 'Bouquet', rich mauve; and 'Alice Hardwicke', rosy-salmon.

The John Innes composts have proved very suitable for many subjects and they are still widely depended upon even although other soil mixtures have come into prominence recently. Their availability means they are a great boon to those who have no facilities for mixing up their own soils, for it is easy to obtain these composts from garden stores and nursery gardens.

Should you wish to make up your own John Innes composts, however, the following are the formulas:

John Innes Compost No 1

2 parts by bulk medium loam.

1 part by bulk good moss peat.

1 part by bulk coarse sand.

Adding to each bushel of this mixture $1\frac{1}{2}$ oz Superphosphate of Lime (16% phosphoric acid) and 1 oz Ground Limestone or Chalk.

John Innes Compost No 2

7 parts by bulk medium loam.

3 parts by bulk good moss peat.

2 parts by bulk coarse sand.

Add to each bushel of this mixture the John Innes base fertiliser made up of: $1\frac{1}{2}$ oz Hoof and Horn meal, $\frac{1}{8}$ in grist (13% nitrogen), $1\frac{1}{2}$ oz Superphosphate of Lime (16% phosphoric acid), $\frac{3}{4}$ oz Sulphate of Potash (48% pure potash) and 1 oz ground Limestone or Chalk.

For subsequent potting as the plants need more feeding, use the John Innes Potting No 3, which contains 3 times the quantity of base fertiliser and ground chalk.

Leaf mould may be used instead of moss peat, and less sand will be required if a light loam is used.

It should be pointed out that it is always better to sift the Superphosphate and Sulphate of Potash through a $\frac{1}{16}$ in sieve before making up the mixture, or before adding the fertilisers to the Compost. Readers should not try to vary the proportions of the fertilisers on their own account. They should be strictly adhered to—not merely approximated—and weighed carefully.

These mixtures may not suit plants which are lime haters. The organic gardener will want to leave out Sulphate of Potash and include another organic ingredient such as Seaweed fertiliser. Others may prefer to replace the artificials with bone meal.

Six

Pests and Diseases

Annual plants are usually comparatively free from pests and diseases. This is not only because they are inherently healthy, but also because their fairly short life gives no opportunity for the building up of disorders which occur with perennial plants.

There is no doubt that if the soil is kept in a healthy condition this will lessen problems. Experiments have clearly shown that where the humus content has been built up, many if not all diseases disappear and pests are less likely to attack. The continued use of chemical or artificial fertiliser will in time produce a thin lifeless site. The use of farmyard manure, compost, spent hops, peat and leaf mould encourages the production of the vital soil organisms which ensure that the plants roots can grow healthily. The soil itself needs enriching and when this is done, much less additional feeding is needed by the plants. Strong balanced growth helps plants to withstand attacks from without and within.

Even so, there are a number of enemies which crop up from time to time and it is wise to learn something about them, so that they may be recognised and dealt with before they do much damage. Much of the battle of trying to kill pests or cure diseases is concerned with being able to diagnose the trouble correctly. Unless we do this, much effort will be wasted. We must suit the remedy to the condition.

Most pests which settle on plants can be killed by stomach poisons which are mostly in the form of liquid sprays or dusts. In the case of slugs and snails, poison baits can be placed near the plants to lure the pests to death. Aphides and other suckers can be destroyed by spraying the plants with Derris, Pyrethrum and Nicotine. The advantage of

Liquid Derris is that it is easily obtainable and non-poisonous to human beings.

Adequate soil drainage does lessen the presence of slugs, snails, millipedes, and leather jackets. There are many predators which do a tremendous amount of good but, unfortunately, they are often carelessly or unknowingly destroyed. These include: insectivorous birds, hedgehogs, frogs, toads, gloworms, ladybirds, hoverflies, lacewings and garden spiders.

In the greenhouse, fumigants and smokes can be used. These are valuable in that they reach the crevices of the structure where pests may be hiding where they cannot be reached by ordinary spraying.

Some pests favour certain subjects, but there are a number which attack all kinds. The following are some of the most common garden pests:

Ants

Not only are these harmful in themselves by disturbing the roots of growing subjects, but they are attracted to plants infested with greenfly which they suck for their sweet excretion. They carry aphids from plant to plant, and are sometimes responsible for the spread of virus diseases. Various insecticides are available, but liquid derris is quite safe, while B.H.C. dust is also effective.

Aphides

There are many species including green fly, black fly, and white fly, which are sometimes called plant lice. They can breed freely on weed plants from which they settle on cultivated subjects. They suck the sap, distort foliage, check growth, and spoil flowers. Often they deposit honeydew thus encouraging ants. If aphids are controlled, ants are rarely much of a problem. Plants should be frequently examined for these pests increase quickly and often settle on the growing points. Regular spraying with a derris-based wash or dust is usually sufficient, although there are several proprietory insecticides. Nicotine and soft soap are effective but need more care in use.

Cockchafers

There are several species of this pest and they are sometimes separated by the common names of May Bug, Garden Chafer and Rose Chafer. When fully developed these blackish-brown beetles are at least an inch long. They usually appear in May and June, when they lay little clusters of eggs below the surface soil. From these hatch fleshy, dirty-white grubs, with brownish-yellow heads. They feed on the roots and lower parts of the stems, causing the plants to wilt and gradually die. These grubs remain in the soil for up to three years before they ultimately develop into beetles and the whole process begins again. The adult beetles will sometimes feed on both leaves and flowers and prove quite destructive. At one time D.D.T. was used to control this pest, but naphthalene, at 4 oz to the sq yd, forked into the soil when it is being turned, will usually clear cockchafers.

Cuckoo Spit

Philaenus spumarius. The frothy mass of cuckoo spit seen on stems and leaves of garden plants conceals the pale yellow nymph of the frog hopper, a jumping insect not more than $\frac{1}{4}$ in long. Ultimately they grow wings and since they can fly, they rapidly spread from plant to plant. Both adults and nymphs suck sap to distort leaves and shoots. To get rid of them, thoroughly spray with water to remove the spittle, then dust with derris or pyrethrum, shaking some on the soil and plants since the pests often fall to the ground and escape.

Cutworms

Cutworms or surface caterpillars are the larvae of several species of moths. These larvae feed at night when they attack the plant stem at or just below ground level, causing growth to collapse. Subjects with fairly thick stems are usually the victims, such as zinnias, marigolds, asters and balsam. The regular moving of the soil around the plants keeps the moth from laying eggs. Where the pests are suspected, examine the soil and the plants, since cutworms are easy to see. This is the surest way of getting rid of them. Alternatively work in naphthalene or paradichlorbenzene at the rate of $\frac{1}{2}$ oz to the square yard.

Earwigs

These sometimes damage foliage and flowers. They are most active at night, hiding under any rubbish lying around. They can be trapped in inverted pots filled with hay or straw, or by one of the proprietory killers.

Eelworm

These cause most damage to bulbous subjects, although sometimes annuals are affected. There are various kinds of eelworm, some of them attacking particular types of plants. They are tiny pests which lay their eggs in the tissues of the plants. Ultimately the plant dies, first exhibiting twisted, stunted growth. Sometimes the pests remain in the soil after particular crops, notably onions and perennial phlox, so care should be taken not to sow annual phlox, gilia and similar subjects immediately after the ground has been occupied by any crop suspected of having had eelworm. In fact, the only way when growing annuals is to starve the ground, since the other method is the hot water system, but this applies only where perennials and bulbous subjects are concerned.

Flea Beetle

Although these very active creatures cause most damage to vegetable crops such as cabbage, turnips and radish they can create trouble among annuals particularly in dry weather. The remedy is to keep the surface soil moving and to give frequent dustings of derris powder.

These pests spend winter hiding in rubbish, appearing in spring to do their damaging work of disfiguring and mutilating the leaves. Eggs are laid on the soil and foliage which allows further broods to hatch.

Keep all weeds, especially shepherd's purse and charlock away from the garden. A firm seed bed will lessen the possibility of attacks in the seedling stages of growth.

Leather Jackets

These are the larvae of the well known Crane Fly or Daddy Longlegs. Most active in grassland, they will attack the roots of annuals and cause distortion, especially on newly broken up ground. They are most prevalent on damp, badly drained soils and if the ground is turned over in winter, birds will often clear the larvae. Naphthalene dusted into the ground 3 oz to the square yard will normally rid the site of these pests.

Millipedes

These are common pests both in the garden and under glass. They usually feed at night, attacking seed-leaves and early growth. They can be distinguished easily from the beneficial centipedes, by their habit of curling up like a spring when disturbed. There are various preparations which may be used on the soil, but the simplest method of getting rid of millipedes, is to trap them with scooped out pieces of potatoes, carrots or turnips, which should be examined daily so the pests can be destroyed.

Slugs and Snails

These are among the most common of garden pests which, if unchecked, can do much damage in a short time. They feed chiefly at night and are indiscriminate in the plants they attack and they persist throughout the winter. They can be found hiding in soil crevices and under stones or rubbish. There are many species of slugs, including the small and large black types, as well as the grey and yellowish sorts. Each slug lays several clusters of eggs which is why they increase so rapidly.

Snails hibernate during winter, hiding under rubbish or in damp places. While it may never be possible to eradicate these pests permanently, their numbers can be greatly reduced by trapping them or using one of the modern slug baits. Large numbers can often be collected during showery weather.

Springtails

These are wingless, active, jumping insects of various shades of colour, such as green, grey and black. They feed on any decaying plant tissues as well as attacking living plants, especially delicate seedlings. This results in the plants becoming malformed and in many cases failing to grow at all. They are less likely to appear in dry weather and as a precaution weeds and refuse should be kept away from the plants since springtails like to hide in such material. If they are suspected, dust around the plants with pyrethrum powder.

Thrips

These tiny insects are unlikely to attack many annuals. Their presence is discovered by silvery markings on the foliage. They are virus carriers, spreading infection by piercing the foliage. Under glass they can be controlled by fumigation. Outdoors, spraying the plants with a nicotine and soft soap wash is usually effective.

Wireworms

These are the larvae of the click beetles and are most destructive soil pests. They attack and spoil a wide range of plants, usually eating the roots, but sometimes they will damage the stems too. They are prevalent in grassland and other land which has not been cultivated, which is why they seem so plentiful on freshly broken up soil. Regular cultivation is the best means of controlling wireworms. They can be trapped by pieces of potato, carrot or turnip placed in the ground, which can be examined frequently so the pests can be destroyed. There are a number of proprietary preparations, most of which contain Gammoxene which can be dusted into the ground when it is being turned.

Woodlice

These are unlikely to be very troublesome on annual plants, but are often present when rubbish is left lying about. They flourish under damp, dull conditions and are often to be found on decaying wood. The remedy is to concentrate on cleanliness. They can be trapped by placing pieces of root vegetables in the surface soil, examining them frequently so the pests can be destroyed.

Diseases which attack annuals

Because of the shortness of the life of annuals they are not prone to so many diseases as perennial subjects. Under good, clean growing conditions and provided first class strains are cultivated, there is no reason to fear disease. Even so, it is well to be aware of the symptoms of possible diseases so that they can be recognised early and dealt with before they gain a hold. While there are several diseases which attack

Ipomoea Morning Glory

almost any species, there are others which settle on particular groups or families.

Botrytis

This is a common trouble of fungus origin appearing both in the open ground and the greenhouse. It is most prevalent in a wet season and under generally damp conditions. It is most likely to settle on plants which are weak and soft growing, while it will flourish where dead and dying plants are left lying about. In the glasshouse, avoid a continuous damp atmosphere. Always encourage firm growth by not over feeding with nitrogen and by including potash in the compost for this encourages sturdiness.

At the slightest sign of the disease appearing, affected plants should be burned. Do not leave them on the surface or the spores will spread. Good drainage will lessen the trouble which is sometimes referred to as grey mould.

Club Root

This trouble is well known as attacking members of the cabbage family. It is of fungus origin and affected roots become swollen and distorted. Apart from its appearance in the vegetable garden, annuals such as candytuft, stocks and alyssum may suffer from club root since they are members of the same cruciferae group or family of plants. Some weeds particularly shepherd's purse and charlock can also be affected by club root. In fact, they often act as hosts for the disease which is one good reason for keeping weeds out of the flower garden. Club root is less likely to appear where the soil contains lime, but immediate protection for the plants can be given by sprinkling 4% calomel dust into the holes when they are made for seedlings. It is wise not to grow susceptible plants in ground which has been cleared of members of the cabbage family.

Damping off

This is another disorder of fungus origin. There are several forms of this disease, some of which have a mildew-like appearance. One of the most common is known as *Pythium de Baryanum*. It chiefly affects seedlings, especially those raised under glass, either before or after the pricking out stage. The tiny plants wither away at ground level and the disease soon spreads to healthy specimens particularly if seedlings remain crowded.

A good, well drained compost and well ventilated situation helps to prevent the disease. Do not over water. Thin sowing is also helpful while when the seedlings are being handled, avoid gripping the tiny stems too firmly, for preference moving the plants by their seed leaves. If the trouble has occurred previously use a solution of Cheshunt Compound on the soil. This will not cure affected plants but will prevent the spread of the disease.

Apart from general diseases there are a few which attack individual families. Chief among these are the following:

Antirrhinum Rust

This fungus covers the stems and undersides of the leaves with rust coloured spores and usually kills the plants. Sometimes affected specimens make fairly good growth and may even flower before collapsing, others wither in a short time. The spraying of the plants with Burgundy mixture helps to keep the disease from spreading, while where the trouble has occurred previously, antirrhinums should not be allowed to overwinter. There are now many rust-resistant varieties.

Aster Blackleg

Sometimes known as Stem Rot, this is another common disease which can soon spoil a batch of plants. The disorder works through the roots, gradually spreading through the entire plant causing crippling growth. Sometimes the plants die quickly. Burn all affected specimens and apply a solution of Cheshunt Compound to the soil in which the remaining asters are growing. Do not grow asters on the same site for a couple of years. A number of wilt resistant varieties are now offered by the leading seedsmen.

Sweet Pea Scorch

This trouble is more likely to occur when plants are grown as single cordons. This method of culture does mean a considerable restriction in the leaf area. The foliage is necessary for the manufacture of chemicals needed for proper growth. Considerable research has been carried out into the question of sweet pea scorch, but so far no definite cause or solution has been discovered. It seems evident, however, that what really happens is that if the plant roots take in the normal amount of feeding matter, they are unable to make use of it all and seek to get rid of the excess quantity through the leaves. This is the cause of the scorch. Sometimes if the plants are mulched and the soil does not dry out, the trouble is only temporary and it might be found helpful to mulch the plants with peat, leaf mould or strawy manure.

Where the trouble has previously occurred, it has been found beneficial to allow each plant to have two leaders instead of one main stem. This is specially so in the case of strong growing varieties.

Virus disease

A few annuals are subject to certain of these and they include nasturtiums, petunias and zinnias. The usual symptoms are stunted, distorted growth and mottling of foliage. All plants suspected of virus should be lifted and burned immediately and if greenfly or other aphis are seen on nearby plants, all should be sprayed with a derris or

Helichrysum Monstrosum mixed

nicotine wash, for aphis often spread diseases as they travel from plant to plant.

Sweet pea mosaic is a virus disease which produces a yellow mottling of the leaves, with discoloured flowers. This condition should not be confused with the mottling of the florets sometimes caused by greenfly, which suck the sap from the flower buds, leading to blotchy colouring when the flowers open. With such greenfly attacks, the foliage does not become discoloured. All plants affected by mosiac should be burned, and the remaining specimens sprayed with a good insecticide to prevent greenfly and other pests from spreading the disease.

Mildew

This is of fungus origin and although slight attacks seem to do little real harm sometimes the white, powder-like growth is very bad, causing a whole batch of plants to become disfigured and useless. Members of the composite or daisy family seem most liable to attacks especially calendulas, although many others, including larkspur and sweet peas, may be attacked and growth crippled.

Mildew in its various forms thrives where the air is damp and the soil dry. As soon as the disorder is seen, dust the plants with yellow sulphur powder or spray with one of the proprietory mildew cures.

Seven

Nomenclature and Glossary

The derivation of all names is given in the dictionary section including those which are a compliment to the plant discoverer or raiser. Names without descriptions are useless and every endeavour has been made to give a true and complete description. Some well known cultivars, which is a modern word for 'cultivated varieties', have turned out upon close inspection and as the result of comparison trials, to be very like other distinguished cultivars. As a matter of accuracy the authentic names are used and at the same time the name by which a cultivar may be more widely known is also indicated.

Height. This is given at the end of each description and indicates the height to which the plants will grow under normal conditions.

Spacing. The average amount of space each plant will occupy is shown and gives an idea of the number of plants needed in a particular area.

Habit. Plants of trailing or climbing habit are marked Tr. or Cl.

Flowering period. The months mentioned are those when the plants are at their best. In the case of foliage subjects, the months are those when they are most showy.

Duration. This is given by the letters after each subject. H.A. indicates hardy annual. H.H.A. half-hardy annual. T.A. tender annual, usually grown in pots in the greenhouse. H.B. hardy biennial, usually grown as an annual. H.H.P. A perennial best grown as an annual.

Half-hardy annuals are those usually grown in warmth early in the year, the seedlings being hardened off before being planted in the garden for a summer bedding display. Hardy annuals are sown where they are to flower, usually in the spring, but in a few cases in the autumn as well.

Any special rooting requirements such as an acid, calcareous, or peaty soil is indicated, otherwise the plants will flourish in ordinary good soil.

Glossary

Alternate	spaced one after another, as with leaves spaced singly at different heights on opposite sides of the stem.
Anther	the part of the stamen containing the pollen.
Awn	a bristle-like appendage found in ornamental grasses.
Bisexual	flowers possessing both stamens and pistils.
Blade	the main or expanded part of the leaf.
Bract	a modified leaf often associated with the flower.
Calyx	the sepals or outer portion of the floral parts.
Capsule	the dry box, pod or fruit containing the seed.
Compound	made up of many parts as in some leaves.
Corymb	a short, broad, flat, top cluster of flowers.
Disk or disc	the central or inner part of 'daisy-like' flowers.
Elongated	stretched out, long as with some leaves.
Filament	the stalk supporting the anther.
Florets	small individual flowers together making a cluster.
Glabrous	smooth with hairs or undulations.
Glaucous	of greyish-white appearance, sometimes bluish-green.
Hirsute	covered with hairs, as in the case of certain foliage.
Imbricated	overlapping in regular order.
Inflorescence	the method of flowering, or referring to the blooms.
Keel	the two lower petals forming a ridge as in sweet peas.
Lateral	on or near the side, secondary.
Mealy	covered with greyish-white powder.
Monoceious	with both male and female flowers produced on the same plant.
Nectar	the sweet fluid secreted by some flowers.
Ovary	the part of the flower which eventually contains the seed.
Panicle	a loose flower cluster, made up of little racemes.
Pedicel	the stalk of an individual flower in a cluster.
Perianth	the calyx and corolla together.
Petaloid	resembling a petal.

Pistil	the female seed bearing organs—ovary style and stigma.
Pistillate	bearing pistils only; female.
Raceme	an indefinite flower cluster.
Radiate	spreading out; arrangement of ray florets.
Ray	the outer florets of 'daisy-like' flowers.
Reflexed	bent slightly downwards or backwards.
Revolute	with tip or margin rolled back.
Rotate	wheel-shaped, used to describe shape of a flower.
Rudimentary	imperfectly developed; immature.
Sac	a pouch; shape of flower.
Scape	leafless stems rising from the ground terminating in a flower.
Segment	a single leaf or petal.
Sepal	one of the separate parts of the calyx.
Sessile	without a stalk; sitting on a leaf.
Spike	an elongated indefinite flower cluster.
Stamen	the male pollen bearing part of the flower.
Striate	marked with fine parallel lines, pencil-like.
Tendril	a long twining extension by which a plant climbs.
Umbel	inflorence in which pedicels arise from the same point.
Whorl	a circular arrangement of parts around an axis at a node.

Eight

Alphabetical list of Annuals

Adonis. A name taken from Greek mythology. The annual varieties from Europe and Asia make charming plants for the border, being especially valuable because of their red, buttercup-shaped flowers, this colour being unusual in annuals. The cut foliage enhances the value of the plant. Sow in spring in warm sunny positions where the plants are to flower.

A. aestivalis from Central Europe is the Pheasant's Eye or Flos Adonis. There is also a yellow form. *A. aleppica* from Syria, is less free flowering and being slower in germinating can, with advantage, be sown in well drained positions in autumn.

A. annua is known as the Autumn Flos Adonis, which is a naturalised plant in parts of England. Its blood-red petals have a black spot at the base.

18 in. Spacing 12 in. June–September. H.A.

Ageratum. From G. ageras, a reference to the long lasting nature of the flowers. Known as the Floss Flower, the modern varieties have been bred from two wild species found in tropical America. They are splendid subjects for bedding out during the summer, having attractive, fluffy flower heads. All grow in good garden soil, preferably in a sunny situation, while they make excellent pot plants.

A. mexicanum is tall growing, often more than 12 in high. It is from this that many of the best known dwarf sorts have come. These include 'Blue Mink', with large trusses of powder blue flowers on compact plants. 'Little Blue Star', pale blue; 'White Cushion', white; and 'Fairy Pink', salmon rose. Recently several new F.1 hybrids have been introduced, especially good being 'North Sea' with beautiful violet-blue flowers.

4–6 in. Spacing 6–8 in. July–October. H.H.A.

Agrostemma. Of European origin this name comes from two words, *agros*, meaning field, and *stemma*, crown. An erect branching plant, the stiff, wiry stems stand up well to winds. It grows well in ordinary soil and prefers a sunny situation. There are several varieties most of which have come from *A. githago*, magenta-red, our native Corn Cockle, which is sometimes offered as lychnis, and *A. coeli-rosa*, rose-pink. The best variety now available is known as 'Milas', producing lilac-pink single flowers with paler centres. Corn Cockles usually seed themselves freely.

2–3 ft. Spacing 9–12 in. June–September. H.A.

Alonsoa. Commemorating a Spanish diplomat, the Mask Flower is a native of Chile and Peru. It grows well in a sunny position. An early flowering summer bedding subject, it also makes a splendid pot plant for the cool greenhouse. Pinch back growth when the plants are 4 in high to encourage shapely development. One of the best species for general purposes is *A. warscewiczii* which makes bushy plants with bright orange-scarlet flowers. Sow in warmth in March or outdoors in May.

15–18 in. Spacing 9–12 in. July–October. H.H.A.

Althaea. From the Greek meaning to heal, a reference to the medicinal qualities of some species. *A. hybrida semperflorens* of garden origin, is the annual Hollyhock. A sowing in warmth in February or March will produce flowering plants from the end of July, or seed sown outdoors in April will bloom later. The single and double flowers are in many beautiful art shades. These annuals are rarely if ever attacked by rust disease which often spoils perennial hollyhocks.

4–5 ft. Spacing 2 ft. August–September. H.A.

Alyssum. This name means 'not madness', in reference to its supposed properties of curing madness in dogs. Of European origin this is a suitable subject for edging, the rockery, or formal bedding. There are many varieties in cultivation, among which are: 'Carpet of Snow', 3 in, pure white flowers. 'Minimum', 2 in, very dwarf, white, excellent for edging. 'Rosie O'Day' is a rose-pink counterpart of Carpet of Snow.

2–10 in. Spacing 6–8 in. June–October. H.A.

Amaranthus. This name comes from the Greek, meaning unfading, indicating the long lasting nature of the blooms. This is a large family of plants from tropical and temperate regions containing widely differing species. Many of them are of great value as foliage plants, particularly the modern sorts such as 'Molten Fire', with glowing variegated purple-bronze and crimson-scarlet foliage. *A. tricolor splendens* is scarlet, splashed yellow and bronze and a good greenhouse pot plant. *Amaranthus caudatus* is notable for its long racemes of flowers giving rise to the common name of Love Lies Bleeding. There are both green and red forms.

2–3 ft. Spacing 18 in. July–September. H.H.A.

Amellus. See *charieis*.

Ammobium. This Australian plant thrives in sandy soil, which is the meaning of its name. It is classed as an everlasting flower, since the blooms can be cut and dried for winter decoration. *A. alatum* has white flowers with prominent golden centres.

1½–2 ft. Spacing 9 in. July–September. H.H.A.

Anagallis. The name of this widely distributed plant is derived from a word meaning to laugh again, in reference to the gay appearance of the little flowers. Their common name is Pimpernel of which there are red, blue and white forms. *Anagallis coerulea*, grows 6 in high and has gentian blue flowers. *A. sanguinea* is deep scarlet.

6–8 in. Spacing 6 in. June–September. H.H.A.

Androsace. The interpretation of the word indicates a buckler, probably because of the shape of the leaves of some species. Often known as Rock Jasmin, there are many species in this family, some being biennials and perennials. The annual forms, coming mostly from Asia, are of simple culture. Attractive little plants for the rock garden and border edgings, they are quite happy in semi-shady places, flourishing specially well where there is leaf mould or other humus matter in the soil. Sowing is best done at different times according to the species grown, although if any are being used for pot work in the greenhouse, seed can be sown in the cool house in February.

A. albana makes rosettes of oval-pointed leaves with tiny pink flowers. If sown in prepared sites in late August or early September, plants will bloom in spring. *A. chaixii* also forms rosettes of pointed leaves and pink flowers. Sow in spring or autumn.

A. macrantha has white flowers. Sow in spring for summer flowering. *A. maxima* with tiny whitish pink flowers can be treated similarly.

4–6 in. Spacing 4–5 in. May–September. H.A.

Anoda. This is a mallow-like plant of Mexican origin. The name literally means, without nodes or joints. Seed should be sown in spring in a sunny position where the plants are to flower.

A. cristata makes a pleasing plant with wide-mounted flowers of lilac pink. There is also a white form. *A. hastata* has lance-shaped greyish leaves and pretty pink flowers.

2–3½ ft. Spacing 15–18 in. June–September. H.A.

Anthemis. See *cladanthus*.

Antirrhinum. The name comes from the Greek meaning nose flower or more literally, snout flower, in reference to the shape of the flowers which have several common titles including Snapdragon or Dragon's Mouth. As in the case of some other well known subjects such as ageratum, lobelia and nicotiana, antirrhinums are strictly speaking perennials. They are usually rejected when entered at most flower shows as annuals, disqualified as being in the wrong class.

While sometimes these plants come through an average winter without much harm, they are frequently affected by cold weather and look so poor and shabby in early spring that most gardeners prefer to treat them as half-hardy annuals, sowing seed under glass fairly early in the year and gradually hardening off the plants so that they can be moved to flowering positions in May. Seed can also be sown in the cold frame in August, the frame lights being put on during the winter with plenty of ventilation given to obtain sturdy growth of good colour.

Antirrhinums grow best on light, neutral or slightly alkaline soils which have been well enriched the previous autumn. Heavier soils can be made suitable by working in plenty of humus matter while a dressing of superphosphates in early spring will encourage the development of a strong fibrous root system so necessary for flower production.

Antirrhinum asarina and *A. glutinosum* are two of the more or less wild European species, both having yellow or cream flowers. It is from *A. majus* the pink 'common' species and native of the Mediterranean regions and now sometimes found naturalised in Britain, that the many garden forms have been developed.

Many of the earlier varieties became affected by rust disease but, as the result of work carried out by the Royal Horticultural Society and some specialist seed growers in Britain and America, a number of good rust resistant varieties are now available. A group of vigorous tall growing sorts has also been perfected. Among these tall *A. majus grandiflora* varieties are: 'Goliath', salmon pink, shaded orange; 'Monarch', crimson; 'Queen Victoria', pure white; and 'Yellow King'. All grow 3 ft high.

Of the *A. majus nanum* sorts 15-18 in high, 'Black Prince', crimson; 'Blaze', coppery-orange; and 'Nelrose', coral pink are particularly good. Tom Thumb bedding varieties are useful for border edgings and grow about 9 in high, usually being available in mixture.

Among the newer rust-resistant sorts are Coral, Scarlet, Yellow, White and 'Orange Monarch' all growing about 18 in. Plant breeders have introduced a number of remarkable F.1 hybrids including the Penstemon flowered, a remarkable new break, the blooms having open petals rather like those of a penstemon. The Double Formula mixed produces large flowers closely spaced on long spikes, the additional petals giving a double effect.

The latest development in tall antirrhinums is the 'Rocket Hybrids' producing very tall base-branching plants in many lovely colours.

6 in–3 ft. Spacing 9–12 in. June–October. H.H.P. treat as H.H.A.

Arctotis. From two Greek words, *arktos* and *ous*, probably in reference to the shaggy seed heads. The quick growth and brilliant colourings of these South African Daisies are the reasons for their popularity. Grown in a light sandy soil and fairly dry, sunny situation, the plants produce flowers over a long period and until frosts arrive.

A. grandis can be raised under glass or sown outdoors in late April where the plants are to bloom. The elegant flowers are a glistening white with a delicate lavender shading on the reverse of the petals, while they have a blue central disc. The grey-green foliage is delicately cut. From crosses with several species, a handsome strain of hybrids has been produced, some being almost a primrose shade.

18 in. Spacing 9–12 in. June–October. C. H.H.A.

A. leptorhiza briziscarpa produces low growing greyish feathery foliage and flowers of varying shades of orange with darker centres.

6–8 in. Spacing 9–12 in. June–October. H.H.A.

Argemone. From *argema*, an allusion to an eye disease which this plant was once said to cure.

Often known as the Prickly Poppy or Yellow Thistle, the subject is native of tropical America. A rapid grower, the freely produced flowers develop quickly from an early spring sowing. There are upwards of a dozen species but *A. grandiflora* is outstanding, with creamy white, poppy-like flowers. The stiff rather prickly foliage is thistle-like. Light soil and a sunny situation leads to the best results. Plants can be raised by sowing seed under glass in February or in the open ground in early April, taking care not to damage the roots when transplanting.

12 in.   Spacing 12 in.   June–September.   H.H.B.

Arenaria. While the perennial varieties are well known, the annual form is rarely grown. The Latin name indicates that this subject is a sand lover which is why it is known as Sandwort. Ordinary soil and a sunny situation suit this plant.

A. groenlandica comes from Greenland and forms tufts which, as the plants grow into each other, make an attractive mat covered with white flowers in summer.

3 in.   Spacing 3–4 in.   July–September.   H.A.

Arnebia. This title is from the Arabic name for the plant which is sometimes known as the Arabian Primrose. This is another easily grown plant which deserves wider cultivation. Seeds can be sown where the plants are to flower, although they can also be germinated under glass in March and the plants placed in their flowering positions in May.

A. cornuta has rather hairy lanceolate leaves and somewhat tubular yellow flowers, each petal being marked with a black or deep maroon spot. As with the perennial species, there is a legend attached to this plant, for it is said that the flower was touched by the prophet Mohammed, leaving his finger print on the petals. Another theory is that the presence of the black spots is an indication of good weather. This is not substantiated by experience.

15–20 in.   Spacing 12 in.   July–September.   H.A.

Artemesia. This is the title of the family of plants and shrubs often referred to as Wormwood. The name comes from Artemis or Diana the Greek goddess. These annuals are of value because of their ferny ornamental foliage. Sow seed in a sheltered place where the plants are to flower, remembering that they produce tall pyramidal growth and so need placing with discretion.

A. annua, an Asian plant, makes really graceful growth with the fresh green foliage being quite sweetly scented. The whitish-yellow flowers are produced in heads, being practically rayless.

5–6 ft.   Spacing 2 ft.   July–September.   H.A.

Atriplex. Sometimes known as *Orach* which is the Latin name, this annual is occasionally grown as a vegetable since the leaves can be cooked and eaten like spinach. Although there is nothing special about the plant, it makes an attractive foliage dot plant for the garden. The red-leaved forms are specially suitable for this purpose. Sow in April or May where the plants are to mature. *A. hortensis* is the green-leaved form which is sometimes eaten as a vegetable. It is *A. hortensis atro-sanguinia (cupreata)* with its crimson leaves, which is so decorative. 4–5 ft.   Spacing 18 in.   July–September.   H.A.

Layia elegans

Avena. This is the classical name for the well known oat. Easy to grow in any good soil, this is not a subject which one would generally recommend for the garden. There is, however, one exception *A. sterilis* which is known as the Animated Oat. This is because when the mature seeds are placed on the ground they will twist and turn as though alive. This action is due to the little beards or awns attached to the seed which are sensitive to atmospheric conditions, particularly humidity. It is a useful subject for including in bouquets both fresh and dried.

2–3 ft. Spacing 6–7 in. July–October. H.A.

Baeria. A little known Californian annual, named after a German zoologist of the nineteenth century. Ordinary, good, well drained soil and a sunny situation suits this plant. *B. coronaria* has attractively cut hairy foliage and freely produced small rich yellow flowers.

B. gracilis, sometimes known as Goldfields, is suitable for the rock garden or front of the border.

6–9 in. Spacing 6 in. June–September. H.A.

Bartonia. See *Mentzelia*.

Bidens. Native to Mexico the name means two tooth, a reference to the shape of the seeds.

A sunny position and ordinary soil is suitable. *B. grandiflora (serrulata)* has yellow, five-petalled flowers. *B. pilosa* has immature-looking white petals creating an odd rather than attractive appearance. There are some half-hardy species a few of which are offered under cosmos.

12-24 in. Spacing 12 in. July–September. H.A.

Borago. This ancient plant now naturalised in parts of Europe, Asia and the Mediterranean regions owes its name to the hairy or shaggy foliage, the title coming from the Latin *burra*. Although it will grow in almost any soil it does seem to do best in a rather dry position. It was a favourite plant when unusual subjects were used in salads and for flavourings, the flowers imparting an aroma to cider and claret cup. It is not without attraction as a garden plant.

B. officinalis has really hairy foliage and rather nodding heads of beautiful blue flowers.

12–24 in. Spacing 12–15 in. June–September. H.A.

Brachycome. Two Greek words mean short hair, in reference to thin hairs on the seeds which give this plant its name. It has the common title of Swan River Daisy. A most dainty subject for edging purposes, it does best in a sunny position. Seed can be sown in April, or, to provide an early spring flowering and pot plants for the greenhouse, sow in early September.

B. iberidifolia produces numerous clusters of cineraria-like flowers of a bluish-purple shade. Several colour selections have been made in shades of blue, white and a less common pink.

9 in. Spacing 6–9 in. June–October. H.A.

Briza. This is an old Greek name for rye. Often known as Quaking Grass, this is an ornamental subject of great value if used with cut flowers and when dried for winter use.

B. maxima has slender rather drooping stems which carry bronze spikelets. *B. minor* (*gracilis*) is very similar but not so tall and of rather daintier appearance.

10–20 in. Spacing 9–10 in. May–September. H.A.

Bromas. This is another ornamental grass suitable for using with cut flowers or for winter decoration. The root meaning of the name is food and it grows almost anywhere.

B. brizaeformis is often known as Quake Grass. It has drooping spikelets not unlike the brizas.

12–20 in. Spacing 9–12 in. July–September. H.A.

Caiophora. See *Loasa*.

Calandrinia. Named after an Italian botanist, this is strictly speaking, a tender perennial but can be grown as an annual. Even in a light soil and sunny position they become very bedraggled in the autumn, which is really why they are best treated as annuals. Fortunately they seed themselves freely and are sometimes known as Rock Purslane.

C. ciliata, menziesii (*speciosa*) has reddish purple flowers which are inclined to close in dull light.

C. umbellata is the most showy with clusters of violet crimson flowers. This species too, closes its flowers in poor light and in the evenings.

6–9 in. Spacing 6–7 in. June–September. H.H.P.

Calceolaria. This title comes from the Latin word *calceus* meaning slipper, a reference to the shape of the flower, which is why this South American plant is sometimes known as Slipperwort.

The perennial varieties are much valued as greenhouse plants but the annual forms are not well known but certainly worth growing. Seed can be sown under glass in March, the seedlings being moved to the outdoor places in late May or early June.

C. mexicana can if preferred be sown shallowly directly outdoors in a sunny position although it will flower in partial shade too. It has bright green, rather hairy leaves and pale yellow flowers. *C. scabiosaefolia* is also pale yellow. In both cases the flowers are, of course, smaller than the greenhouse species.

12 in.   Spacing 9–10 in.   July–September.   H.H.A.

Calendula. From the Latin *calendae*, meaning the first day of the month, an allusion to the continuous flowering character of this plant. A native of Southern Europe it is often known as the garden or Pot Marigold. The flowers were once used by herbalists in soups for their good effects on the heart, although they are rarely so used to-day.

A very hardy plant it often seeds itself almost too freely. This subject likes light soil and plenty of sun, but can often be found thriving profusely under the reverse conditions. Can be sown in spring or autumn.

Mentzelia aurea

Calendula officinalis is the species which originally came to this country but there are now scores of good sorts in cultivation. Reliable varieties include: 'Campfire', deep orange; 'Chrysantha', canary yellow; 'Geisha Girl', glowing orange with a reddish sheen to the incurving petals; 'Lemon Queen'; and Double Art Shades, taking in blendings varying from soft cream to deep orange with dark centres.

18–24 in. Spacing 12 in. April–October. H.A.

Callirrhoe is a little known subject belonging to the mallow family. A native of North America it is named after one of the Greek gods. Sow seed in April where the plants are to flower.

C. pedata has freely produced, reddish purple hollyhock-like flowers.

3 ft. Spacing 24–30 in. August–October. H.A.

Callistephus which means beautiful crown, is the botanical title for the China aster which naturally, is a native of China and also Japan, being introduced to Britain about 1731. There are many types and sections now available, all apparently having been developed from *C. hortensis*, also known as *C. chinensis*, said to have been introduced to Europe by a missionary. This is a single flowered species, and from it have sprung innumerable single and double strains, providing a wonderful display during summer and autumn. Most are first class for cutting.

Seed of all asters can be sown throughout April. Use trays, pans or boxes of the John Innes seed compost, or something similar. Sow thinly and evenly with only a slight covering of soil over the seed. Cover the boxes with glass after sowing, but remove it once the seedlings appear. When pricking out, handle the plants with care, never overwater, but do not let the soil dry out. A sunny situation should be chosen for the aster bed, which should be prepared as soon as possible, making sure that drainage is good. Planting outdoors is usually possible in May. Asters make excellent pot plants for flowering from October onwards. For this purpose sow seed in the cold frame in June and transfer the plants to the cool greenhouse in September.

C. hortensis takes in all the florist's varieties. Now they are often placed in separate groups according to their characteristics and seedsmen's catalogues will reveal a tremendous, almost bewildering range of named sorts. It is therefore very convenient that they have been divided into sections, each with its particular characteristics.

The fairly recently introduced 'Super Princess' strain has large, fully double blooms, the petals quilling towards the centre. 'Duchess Asters' also have strong rigid stems, the large flowers looking like incurving chrysanthemums, making them most valuable. They are available in separate colours such as yellow, pink, blue and rose while the mixture gives a striking display.

Giant Comet asters have elegant flowers resembling Japanese chrysanthemums. From this strain has come the giant branching 'Comet' or Crego asters. These have branching stems up to 2½ ft long, with the typical curled and fluffy looking flowers.

Ostrich Plume, or Feather asters, have long been used for decorative purposes. The improved strains, with their long stems and feathery recurving petals, never fail to cause attraction. They are available in several colours, such as crimson, blue, rose and white, as well as mixtures.

Californian Giant or 'Perfection' asters, are truly magnificent, producing loosely arranged shaggy petals similar to giant chrysanthemums, on long, strong stems of 2½ ft or so. From this strain has come the Super Giant varieties, 'El Monte', crimson and 'Los Angeles', shell-pink, of which the flowers are very large indeed.

The Mammoth Victorian strain, is a very great improvement on the old mid-season type. The very large, ball-shaped, double flowers have overlapping petals on strong stems.

Chrysanthemum flowered asters are of dwarf, compact habit, ideal for bedding. Apart from the mixture, the variety 'Thousand Wonders' (*Tausendschon*) with pale rose-pink flowers, and 'Chasters Erfurt', with deeper rose flowers, are noteworthy both for edging and growing in pots or window boxes.

The Colour Carpet strain also produces chrysanthemum-like flowers in shades of blue, pink and red, being ideal for bedding and edging, with the added attribute of being wilt resistant.

'Queen of the Market' asters are very early, with branching stems of 15–20 in high. This is a suitable strain for market growers being very useful for cutting.

Eclipse or Ray asters are most elegant and graceful having quilled petals making the flowers valuable for indoor decoration.

Powderpuff asters are of compact habit specially suitable for cutting since the flowers do not show an eye or yellow centre. The upright growth allows close spacing, as little as 5–8 in being sufficient, resulting in a ribbon of colour.

Paeony-flowered varieties have flowers like incurved chrysanthemums on long strong stems.

Anemone flowered is the name of a small group of varieties having an outer ring of longish petals and a quilled centre giving the effect of a double anemone.

The 'Unicum' quilled strain is particularly good. The large double flowers have long slender petals on strong stems. Their dainty appearance makes them ideal for all decorative purposes. Named varieties include: 'Filigran', salmon-apricot, reminding one of a cactus dahlia; 'Citron', deep cream; 'Silvery Blue', charming silvery-blue and 'Edelstein', large pure white.

Pompone asters are attractive. 'Pirette', is cerise coloured, 'Puck', violet-blue, and 'Blue Domino', purple-mauve, all having a white centre and produced on upright, branching stems. These as well as the dwarfer growing 'Waldersee' mixture, can be lifted when in flower and brought indoors.

9–24 in. Spacing 6–12 in. July–September. H.H.A.

Centaurea. A name taken from Greek mythology. There are various European species but *C. cyanus* is the most grown, having the popular name of Cornflower and known also as Blue Bottle and Bluet. First class as a cutting subject, it will flourish almost anywhere, but does not transplant well. Colours available include: blue, pink, white, and flowers tipped with a contrasting shade. Dwarf forms 12 in tall.

2½–3 ft. Spacing 12–18 in. June–October. H.A.

Centaurea moschatus (Musk Scented) is the Sweet Sultan, with large thistle-like, pale lilac-purple heads. There are now yellow, purple, pink and white forms, all sweetly scented and excellent as long lasting cut flowers. *C. imperialis* is the giant Sweet Sultan, taking in the same colours as *C. moschatus*.

18 in. Spacing 12 in. July–September. H.A.

Charieis. This showy South African plant is often known and catalogued under kaulfussia. The word charies is descriptive since in Greek it means elegant.

Seed can be sown in the open ground where the plants are to bloom choosing a sunny position, or for very early flowering, sowings may be made under glass in March, the seedlings being moved to their final quarters once they can be handled easily. This subject is also a splendid pot plant for the cool greenhouse, several specimens in a 6 or 7 in pot looking really superb.

C. heterophylla (*Kaulfussia amelloides*) forms· compact plants and freely produces bright blue, daisy-like flowers usually with yellow centres, although sometimes, these are a bluish shade. The soft downy leaves are grey-green. Varieties include *atroviolacea*, very dark blue; and *kermesina*, violet-red.

5–6 in. Spacing 6 in. June–September. H.A.

Chenopodium. This is the name of quite a large family of plants coming from various parts of the world. The majority are perennials, some being grown for their edible qualities. A few are annuals with decorative foliage useful for backgrounds or as dot plants.

Seed should be sown in March in flowering positions. Once plants have been grown, self-sown seedlings will often appear annually. Best results come where the seed does not dry out at any time.

C. botrys (*ambrosia*) has well cut aromatic foliage with feathery spikes of scented reddish flowers. It has the common name of Feathered Geranium.

C. purpurascens from China, forms clusters of small red flowers the leaves having a powdery appearance. There is also a variegated form.

2–3 ft. Spacing 12–15 in. July–October. H.A.

Chickling Vetch. See *Lathyrus*.

Clarkia, named after Capt. W. Clarke an American explorer, are among the most useful and popular of all annual flowers. Seed is best sown where the plants are to flower since seedlings do not transplant well. For preference, select a light soil.

They make excellent pot plants for spring flowering in the cool greenhouse if seed is sown in early September. There are a number of species, some of which are sometimes listed under the eucharidiums.

C. pulchella has flowers varying in colour from lilac to white, with rather cut-edged petals.

C. elegans from California is the parent of most of the double garden varieties. It has large purple flowers carried on reddish stems with fairly broad leaves, while the petals are not cut. Of the many fine named varieties in cultivation the following are most reliable. 'Albatross', white; 'Enchantress', double salmon-pink; 'Lady Satin

Rose', double rose-pink; 'Orange King', orange-scarlet; and 'Vesuvius', orange-scarlet.

18–24 in.   Spacing 12 in.   June–September.   H.A.

Clary. See *Salvia horminum*.

Claytonia. Named in honour of John Clayton, a botanist of Virginia, this is a genus of low growing or trailing plants most useful for the rock garden. *C. siberica* sometimes known as the Siberian purslane, produces palish rose-pink flowers. It is excellent for the lower regions of an alpine garden, since it flourishes in damp, peaty soil. It can sometimes be found naturalised in parts of Britain.

6 in.   Spacing 9–12 in.   June–September.   H.A.

Cleome. A name of uncertain origin. Native of the Southern states of America, this subject has the common name of Spider plant because of the unusual way in which flowers are produced. Clusters of four-petalled flowers develop at the top of the stems, the long stamens giving a spidery effect. *C. spinosa*, purple, although often emitting an unpleasant scent, is a striking plant, both stems and leaves being armed with spines. *C. gigantea* is rather taller growing, the greenish white flowers having prominent pink stamens.

4–6 ft.   Spacing 3 ft.   July–September.   H.H.A.

Clintonia. See *Downingia*.

Collinsia. Named after Zaccheus Collins an American Naturalist, 1764–1831. These easily grown hardy annuals can be sown where they are to bloom. They look well in the mixed border or when used as an edging. Sown in autumn they make bushier earlier flowering plants, than from the more usual spring sowings.

C. bicolor (*heterophylla*) from California has clusters of whitish flowers shaded rosy-lilac or purple. There are several forms with salmon, rose and lilac blooms.

C. bartsiaefolia is white with a lower lip of lilac. *C. grandiflora* has larger flowers, in this case the lower lip being deep blue.

12–14 in.   Spacing 6–8 in.   June–September.   H.A.

Collomia. From a Greek word meaning 'glue', a reference to the sticky substance surrounding the seeds, this looks best when sown in little groups. Spring sowing is usual but in sheltered positions sowing can be done in September to obtain earlier flowering plants. A good bee plant.

C. coccinea, also known as *C. cavanillesii* and *C. lateritia*, comes from South America and has clusters of five-petalled scarlet flowers. It is sometimes catalogued as *Gilia coccinea*.

C. grandiflora is less common, having narrow tubular flowers varying in colour from buff to salmon.

18–24 in. Spacing 12 in. July–September. H.A.

Cladanthus. In Greek, this name simply means a flower. Native of Spain and Morocco this subject is sometimes included in the genus anthemis. A splendid plant for the annual border, the large, golden-yellow flowers are surrounded by pale green feathery foliage. Strong growing and rarely needing supports, the plants have foliage and flowers which are pleasantly scented.

A light soil in a warm sunny situation suits these plants. Sow seed in March where the plants are to flower.

C. arabacus (*Anthemis arabica*) comes from Arabia and is a first-class border plant, the freely produced, bright yellow flowers looking especially attractive against the finely cut, fern-like foliage.

12–15 in. Spacing 9–12 in. July–September. H.A.

Cnicus. From a Greek word meaning to vex, a reference to the plants being prickly. Most members of this family are perennials, but *C. benedictus* is one of the few annual forms which are sometimes referred to as the Blessed Thistle. The terminal heads of yellow flowers are surrounded by bristly bracts.

24 in. Spacing 12–15 in. July–October. H.A.

Convolvulus. From the Latin to entwine. An easily grown family of plants chiefly from Mediterranean regions. Not to be confused with the so called climbing convolvulus of which the proper name is ipomaea or Quamoclit.

All like light soil and sun. A great advantage the annuals have is that they do not become a nuisance as do some of the perennial forms frequently known as Bindweed, which have such strong persistent invasive roots.

C. elongatus produces small white funnel-shaped flowers well set off by the oval or heart-shaped leaves.

C. tricolor often listed as *C. minor*, is the most widely grown. It has flowers of bright blue with a yellowish throat. There are now many good varieties or forms of this species including 'Cambridge Blue', 'Royal Ensign', bright ultramarine blue; 'Royal Marine', deep blue, and 'Lavender Rosette', which has grey green foliage. All are most effective if planted in groups.

6–12 in. Spacing 7–10 in. June–October. H.A.

Cobaea. Of Mexican origin this name commemorates Senor Cobo, a Spanish priest and botanist of the seventeenth century. The large, flattish seeds should be sown in pots in warmth in March. The plants can be grown in the greenhouse or, after hardening off, can be planted outdoors in light soil in a sheltered position where they are excellent for covering fences and trellis work to which they cling with their strong tendrils. *C. scandens* a rapid grower sometimes referred to as Jack Beanstalk. The large, bell-shaped flowers are first a greenish colour and then turn to violet-purple, often marked green with protruding style and stamens. This plant has the common names of Cathedral Bells and Cup and Saucer plant.

10–20 ft. Spacing 5–6 ft. July–October. Cl. H.H.P.

Coix. Of Asian origin, this is an ornamental grass of value, the name coming from Greek. Seed can be sown where the plants are to grow or seedlings transplant well if started in pans. *C. lachryma-jobi* is of special interest, because of the ornamental seeds produced. These are often up to $\frac{1}{4}$ in in diameter resembling pearly-grey beads, which look like tears. This is why the specific name was given, for this literally means 'Job's Tears'. It is said the seeds were once used in tropical countries for making up rosaries or necklaces. There is also an uncommon form with striped leaves.

24 in. Spacing 9 in. July–September. H.H.A.

Coreopsis. From two Greek words meaning resemblance of the seeds to a bug, hence the common name of Tickweed. Coming chiefly from North America these annual species and varieties are often listed by seedsmen as calliopsis, although there is no authority for so doing. Excellent garden plants, coreopsis will grow in ordinary, often quite poor soil. They look fine in large groups when used in a mixed border where they can be sown in their flowering positions. They can also be sown under glass in March for planting outdoors in May.

As a result of selection and hybridization, there are now both dwarf and taller growing varieties. *C. drummondii* is a fine species with golden yellow petals having a dark purple central disc surrounded by a brownish ring. It has several forms varying in depth of colour.

83

C. tinctoria sometimes known as *C. bicolor* and *C. elegans*, has bright yellow petals enhanced by a crimson brown zone. From this has come many named varieties as offered in seedsmen's catalogues. These are mostly in shades of yellow but a few, such as 'The Garnet', have crimson-scarlet flowers, while some are speckled or striped.

9–24 in.   Spacing 6–10 in.   June–October.   H.A.

Cornflower. See *Centaurea cyanus*.

Corn Marigold. See *Chrysanthemum segetum*.

Cosmos. This name is from the Greek *kosmos*, ornament, a tribute to the beauty of the flowers. Sometimes listed as Cosmea, these plants have delicately-cut foliage as well as dainty flowers. Although they can be sown outdoors in May, it is best to start them in gentle

Molucella laevis

heat in February to obtain early flowering. Fine plants for the back of the border, they flower for many weeks during the summer and autumn. *C. bipinnatus* from Mexico has single flowers of lilac-purple and it is from this species that most garden varieties have been derived. There are rose-pink, white or dark-centred pink sorts. There are also some excellent double and crested flowering sorts. *C. sulphureum* has golden-yellow flowers and is the parent of most of the modern yellow and orange flowers.

3–5 ft. Spacing 18–24 in. July–October. C. H.H.A.

Cream Cups. See *platystemon*.

Crepis. From the Greek meaning sandal, a somewhat obscure reference, possibly referring to the shape of the leaves. Often known as Hawkweed, this is an easily grown annual with no special requirements, which should be sown where it is to flower.

C. rubra from Southern Europe, produces many dandelion-like heads of pink flowers, being excellent for the rock garden or front of the border. There is also a white form.

12–15 in. Spacing 6–7 in. June–September. H.A.

Cuphea. From the Greek *kyphos*, curved, supposedly in reference to the form of the seed capsule. These tender Mexican plants are usually grown in pots in the greenhouse, but are sometimes used outdoors as summer bedding plants. For this purpose sow seed under glass in March and after the seedlings have been hardened off, move them to their flowering places in June. There are several species in cultivation specially reliable being *C. miniata*, which forms little bushes of delicate leaves and sprays of red flowers having green and purple calyces, and *C. ignea* (*platycentra*), known as the Cigar Plant. It has bright scarlet tubes, but no actual petals. At the end of each tube is a dark ring which, with a white mouth, gives the resemblance to a cigar.

12 in. Spacing 9 in. July–September. T.A.

Cynoglossum. In Greek this name means 'Dog's Tongue' in reference to the form and texture of the leaves. This eastern Asian plant, sometimes known as Hound's Tongue and the Chinese Forget-me-not, is strictly a biennial, but is usually treated as an annual. Seed is sown under glass in March, the seedlings being transplanted outdoors in May, or sowings can be made in the open at the end of April.

C. amabile, as the name suggests, is lovely, with downy foliage and pleasing sprays of turquoise-blue. It has a number of named forms with deep blue, pale blue, white or rose-pink flowers. Excellent for garden decoration, these flowers are of little use when cut since they do not last well.

18–24 in.   Spacing 9–12 in.   July–October.   H.B.

Datura. This is the Arabic name for a group of plants usually grown in the greenhouse but which can be planted outdoors in warm sheltered places. These plants produce large trumpet-shaped flowers, often sweet-scented and a generous supply of foliage.

D. metel, sometimes known as *D. fastuosa* and *D. cornucopia* has the common name of Horn of Plenty, the white flowers, often 6 in long, being shaded purple on the exterior. There are several forms of this species including those with yellow, greenish-yellow and yellowish-purple flowers.

D. meteloides or *Wrightii*, white suffused purple, will often survive the winter and must therefore be regarded as a perennial, although it is usually grown as a half-hardy annual.

3 ft.   Spacing 18–24 in.   July–October.   H.H.A.

Delphinium. This name comes from Dolphin on account of the similarity of the shape of the spur to a dolphin. Natives of Europe and other temperate regions, the Annual Delphiniums are usually known as Larkspur, among the most elegant and useful garden flowers.

Seed may be sown where the plants are to bloom, either in spring or autumn. Germination may be slow especially in dry weather. Thin out the seedlings so that the plants have ample room to develop properly. They do not transplant well. Sun and a fairly rich, moist soil is conducive to free flowering.

D. ajacis with flowers ranging in shades of blue, pink and white, is known as the Rocket Larkspur. From this have come many named varieties all producing branching spikes, and taking in such named sorts as Rosamond, double deep rose and Los Angeles, salmon pink.

D. consolidata is a branching plant, the parent of the so-called, stock-flowered Larkspurs, with fully double blooms in many shades. A form known as 'Giant Imperial' is of more compact habit and is now available in named varieties in separate colours.

2–3 ft.   Spacing 9 in.   June–September.   C.   H.A.

Dianthus. From the Greek meaning divine flower, it is highly valued for its elegance, charm and fragrance. It likes a sunny situation and a light, moderately rich soil where it will bloom profusely.

D. armeria, a native of Great Britain is known as the Deptford Pink producing clusters of small, fringed, deep pink flowers marked white. *D. barbatus*, 'Sweet Wivelsfield', is a garden hybrid carrying flowers in a wide colour range. *D. heddewigii* is also of garden origin and sometimes known as *D. chinensis* or the Indian Pink. A fairly new variety named Bravo has single scarlet flowers carried well above the foliage and there are also some new dwarf strains available.

9–15 in. Spacing 9–10 in. July–October. H.H.A.

Diascia, from the Greek meaning to adorn indicating the showiness

Nigella Persian Jewels

of the flowers. This South African plant deserves greater recognition. Of easy culture, growing well in any good garden soil these diascias like a sunny situation, while they are attractive as pot plants for the cool greenhouse.

Sow under glass in March and early April and transplant to flowering positions outdoors in May.

D. barbarae, sometimes known as Twinspur because each dainty coral-pink flower has two curved spurs or pouches. A form of this, Salmon Queen, has beautiful salmon-pink flowers.

12 in.   Spacing 8–10 in.   June–October.   Pots.   H.H.A.

Didiscus. See *Trachymene*.

Dimorphotheca. The name indicates that two forms of the seed vessels are produced. This splendid African Daisy known as the Star of the Veldt and Corn Marigold is very free flowering, the brilliant colours making the plants most effective in beds or borders. They flourish in good, well drained soil, preferably on the light side. Sun is needed for the flowers to open fully. In dull weather and in the evening the petals close.

Sow in the open ground in April where the plants are to flower and thin the seedlings to allow for full development. Transplanting is not usually very successful. Seed can also be sown directly into pots for greenhouse decoration.

D. aurantiaca, the Namaqualand Daisy, is the best known although there is some doubt as to the name of the plant as listed by seedsmen. It seems likely that this title is actually given to *D. aurantiaca hybrida*, the result of crossing *D. sinuata* and *D. pluvialis* which produces flowers varying in colour from salmon, orange, apricot, to buff and white.

D. pluvialis has large white flowers with green disc, the back of the petals being marked violet. *D. sinuata (calendulacea)* has really large bright orange flowers. It has several forms some having petals marked brown or bronze.

12–15 in.   Spacing 12 in.   June–September.   P.   H.H.A.

Downingia. Named after an American horticulturist, this subject is sometimes known as clintonia. Although rather delicate looking, when grown in sheltered positions in the rock garden or front of the border they are quite attractive. Seed should be sown on the site, subsequently being thinned out as necessary. They can also be grown in pots in the cool greenhouse. *D. elegans* has lobelia-like blue flowers with a white lip. *D. pulchella* is similar, although there is yellow on the lip markings. The plants are useful in pots or hanging baskets since they make little trailing growths.

6–9 in. Spacing 6 in. June–September. H.H.A.

Dracocephalum. The name comes from the shape of the flowers, hence the common name of Dragon's Head. Most of the species are perennial but *D. moldavica* is an annual, from North Europe, bearing leafy stems of open mouthed, violet-blue flowers. An excellent bee plant, both flowers and foliage are scented, the latter having an aroma like lemon-scented balm.

15–20 in. Spacing 1 ft. July–September. H.A.

Eccremocarpus. The name refers to the hanging seed pods. Often known as the Chilean Glory Vine, it is really a tender perennial climber but is almost always treated as an annual. Sow the seed in warmth in February or March giving the plants protection until they can go outdoors where they should have some support, in a sunny situation. It looks well in the cool greenhouse.

E. scaber has clusters of tubular orange-scarlet flowers while there are yellow and red forms.

8–10 ft. Spacing 2 ft. July–September. H.H.A.

Echium. This name comes from the Greek meaning viper, the seed being shaped like a viper's head. This easily grown, free flowering plant sometimes known as Viper's Bugloss is an excellent bee plant quite useful for poor and even dry soils. Native of Southern Europe, they really deserve to be more widely grown. *E. plantagineum* produces sprays of flowers of which the colours are blue and purple. Various selections from this species have been made and one known as 'Blue Bedder' forms compact plants of bright blue. E. Dwarf hybrids takes in a charming colour range including rose, pink, salmon, light blue, lavender and purple.

12 in. Spacing 15–18 in. July–September. H.A.

Emilia. This is a commemorative name of a plant from the tropics also known as Cacalia with the common name of Tassel Flower. It grows in ordinary soil, succeeding in dry sandy situations. Sow where the plants are to flower and thin out according to space available.

E. sagittata or *E. flammea* is often referred to as *Cacalia coccinea* with the colloquial name of Flora's Paint Brush. It is a beautiful plant with clustered heads of bright orange scarlet flowers like small tassels. There is a form known as lutea with yellow flowers. *E. sonchifolia* from India has loose heads of flowers in shades of pink, purple, blue and white.

9 in. Spacing 6–7 in. June–September. H.A.

Emmenanthe. The interpretation of this name 'enduring flowers' indicates its long lasting qualities. Coming from the U.S.A. it is known as Californian Whispering Bells. An uncommon subject it needs sun and a light soil. It can also be sown in pots. *E. penduliflora* carries hanging, bell-shaped, golden flowers which when they become dry rustle in the wind, causing them to 'whisper'.

9–12 in. Spacing 6–8 in. June–September. T.A.

Erigeron. The name literally means 'old man in spring', probably referring to the fact that the leaves of some of the very early kinds are covered with white hairs. A native of the U.S.A. this is a useful plant for the rock garden and is best grown in groups.

E. divergens has small but freely produced lavender-mauve flowers.

12–15 in. Spacing 9 in. June–September. H.A.

Erysimum. Sometimes known as Blister Cress, an allusion to the Greek for this name, which literally means, 'to draw blisters', since some of the species are said to disperse blisters. This subject is closely related to the Wallflower. There are a number of biennial and perennial species but *E. perofskianum* from Afghanistan, is an annual with showy bright orange flowers which look superb when planted in large drifts.

12–15 in. Spacing 12 in. June–October. H.A.

Eschscholtzia. Named in honour of the German naturalist (1793–1831) and grown in Britain since 1826, this annual is often known as the Californian Poppy. It flourishes in light soils in sunny situations and does not need rich rooting conditions. Sow in April where the plants are to bloom for they do not transplant well. Seed can also be sown outdoors in well drained soil in September when they will then flower from early April onwards. Few, if any, annuals can surpass eschscholtzias for their brilliant colourings.

E. caespitosa is a dwarf species growing only 5 or 6 in high, being ideal for the rock garden where the lemon-yellow flowers and grey-green foliage looks attractive.

E. californica has flowers varying from lemon to deep yellow. From this species has come several improved strains including the

Double Art Shades. The range of named varieties is very wide, some having prettily fluted petals in many colours.

12–15 in. Spacing 12 in. June–September. H.A.

Eucharidium. This name means good and agreeable, in praise of the beauty of the plants. A small genus, greatly resembling clarkias, it is now included under that name by some authorities. This easily grown plant likes the sun and a well drained situation, the seed being sown in the open ground in early April.

E. breweri has large rosy-purple scented flowers and is known as Fairy Fans because of the shape of the petals. *E. concinnum* is less common, its petals of rose-pink being deeply cut, giving the flowers the common name of Red Ribbons. *E. grandiflorum* is perhaps the best known. This has rosy-purple flowers, while it has white and pink forms.

12–18 in. Spacing 12 in. July–August. H.A.

Eucnide. The small hairs which cover the leaves give this subject its name. It is, however, better known under Bartonia or Mentzelia and sometimes Microsperma too.

Outdoors it needs a warm sheltered position. It is grand as a greenhouse pot plant and for this purpose, sow in a temperature of 60–65°F in February or March and pot on the seedlings until they reach 5 in pots.

The one species retained here, *E. bartonioides*, is a compact annual from the western United States. This has toothed hairy leaves and large deep golden-yellow flowers with prominent yellow stamens, for which reason the plant is sometimes known as the Golden Tassel.

12–15 in. Spacing 12 in. June–September. H.H.A.

Euphorbia. A classical name given in honour of Euphorbus, physician to a King of Mauritania. This is a large and diverse genus of plants known as spurges. Most species are perennial, some are biennial, and a few annual. Some of these are best grown in the wild garden. *E. lathyrus*, the Caper Spurge, has long, narrow blue-green symmetrically arranged leaves. A secretion in the roots is said to repel moles. *E. heterophylla* is known as the Annual Poinsettia and Fire on the Mountains. Forming a compact bushy plant, it has deep green leaves, the upper ones being marked with vivid scarlet. *E. marginata* or Snow on the Mountains has light green leaves, edged and veined white. The flowers of all species are insignificant.

2–3 ft. Spacing 12 in. July–October. H.H.A.

Eustoma. A name originating in North America. This subject was once grown quite extensively as a pot plant and is sometimes known as Lisianthus, a common name being Prairie Gentian.

Seed should be sown under glass in February and the plants pricked off into small pots and given more room according to growth. Water with care to avoid damping off. Light shade and a fairly humid atmosphere in summer is helpful.

E. russellianum has oval grey-green leaves and large, bell-shaped, blue-purple flowers, each with a dark centre. These flowers remain in good condition for a long time making them useful for cutting.

Eutoca. See *Phacelia.*

Exacum. There is doubt concerning the origin of this name although it was used by Pliny. It is a sub-tropical subject, splendid for the cool greenhouse. Seed should be sown shallowly in early spring in a temperature of 60–65°F. Growth is sometimes slow at first. Light shading from direct sunshine is essential.

E. affine is often of biennial habit but is treated as an annual. The light blue flowers are sweetly scented as are those of the form known as atrocaeruleum which also has attractive yellow stamens. *E. zeylandicum,* from Ceylon, has lance-shaped leaves and clusters of large sky-blue flowers.

12–24 in. July–October. Pots. G.A.

Fagopyrum. This is the Greek for buckwheat given to this subject because the seeds resemble small beech or fagus nuts, the English Buckwheat probably coming from the German buche or beech. Although of little use as an ornamental plant, it is sometimes grown by beekeepers and for providing bird seed, while it is also used when young for digging in as green manure.

F. esculentum (sagittatum) has heart-shaped leaves and clusters of scented pink and white flowers.

18 in. Spacing 9–12 in. July–September. H.A.

Felicia. Although this subject is said by some to commemorate a German officer named Felix, other authorities believe the name is derived from the Latin felix, meaning happy, an allusion to the cheerful appearance of the flowers. There are several splendid annuals in this genus of South African plants which flourish in light soil in a sunny situation being excellent for edging or the rock garden. Sow seed where the plants are to flower or they can be sown under glass and transplanted later.

F. adfinis has large deep blue daisy flowers and makes a good pot plant. *F. amelloides*, mid-blue, is actually a perennial but is often treated as a half-hardy subject. *F. bergeriana*, the Kingfisher Daisy is an attractive low growing species having bright blue flowers with golden centres. *F. fragilis* (*Aster tenellus*) is light blue with narrow foliage.

6–12 in. Spacing 6 in. June–October. H.H.A.

French Marigold. See *Tagetes patula*.

Gaillardia. From M. Gaillard, a French patron of Botany. Easily grown plants of American origin, they provide valuable cut flowers which last a long time in water. Sow under glass in March and transplant outdoors in early May. In sheltered, well-drained places seed can be sown outdoors in September. *G. amblyodon*, a Texan species, has blood-red flowers. *G. pulchella* is a useful species with crimson-purple blooms tipped yellow. It is from this that the best named strains have been developed. These include *Picta*, coppery-red, tipped yellow and *Picta*, 'Indian Chief', bronze-red. *G. picta*, 'lorenziana' is available in mixture, the ray florets being enlarged to give the flower a globular appearance. There are also separate named varieties of this type. A tetraploid strain has been evolved, the very large single flowers being almost as big as those of the perennial gaillardia.

15–18 in. Spacing 10–12 in. July–October. H.H.A.

Gamolepsis. A South African plant with daisy-like flowers. Its name comes from two Greek words referring to the union of the scales underneath the flower heads. An excellent little plant for edging borders or for general display, this greatly resembles the better known tagetes. It succeeds in quite poor soil but should have plenty of sun. Sow seed under glass in March or in open ground at the end of April.

G. tagetes (*annua*) has golden yellow flowers an inch in diameter, the branching stem bearing finely divided leaves.

6–10 in. Spacing 9 in. July–September. H.A.

Gaura. Coming from North America, the name means 'superb'. Although by no means a striking plant, it is useful for the garden border or the cool greenhouse. A well drained, fairly sheltered position and plenty of sun suits this subject. Strictly speaking most species of gaura are perennials but nearly always they are treated as annuals. *G. coccinea* has lance-shaped leaves and spikes of pink, scarlet or white

93

flowers. *G. lindheimeri* is a graceful species having long sprays of white flowers each measuring ¾ in diameter. ∴

2–3 ft. Spacing 12 in. July–October. H.H.P.

Gentiana. Named after Gentius, King of Illyria, who was said to have used the roots of Gentians medicinally. Best known as perennials with marvellous blue flowers, there are a few annual species well worth cultivation. Seed should be sown very shallowly in flowering positions in September or March. The covering of autumn sown seedlings with cloches in severe weather reduces possibility of losses.

G. amarella (*germanica*) has lovely pale blue flowers ½ in long and does best in light shade where the soil does not dry out. *G. campestris* has stalkless leaves and erect, funnel-shaped purple flowers. *G. termalis* is deep blue with lighter shading and likes moist soil in a warm, sheltered place.

3–6 in. Spacing 6–8 in. July–October. H.A.

Gilia. Commemorating Felipe L. Gil, a Spanish botanist. Native of temperate and sub-tropical America, this is a showy easily grown annual. Most species are best sown directly into their flowering places in the open where they like a light, well drained situation. Sown in April, the plants flower from July onwards but for very early blooms, seed can be sown in September.

G. abrotanifolia has very divided foliage and clusters of pale blue, funnel-shaped flowers. *G. capitata* is the best known species, making an excellent pot plant, having clusters of light blue flowers. Selected strains bear larger blooms while there is a white form. *G. lutea* is now listed as *Leptosiphon lutea*. *G. rubra*, often known as *G. coronopifolia* is frequently of perennial habit but is usually treated as an annual. It has exceedingly fine foliage with slender terminal clusters of scarlet, trumpet-shaped flowers and makes a splendid pot plant.

2–2½ ft. Spacing 12 in. June–October. H.A.

Githopsis. The origin of this name is uncertain. Coming from California it is an attractive subject for the rock garden or for border edging. It grows well in moist soils and likes plenty of sun. Sow where the plants are to flower.

6 in. Spacing 4–6 in. July–September. H.A.

Glaucium. This name means glaucous-green, a reference to the colour of the foliage. Sometimes known as the Horned Poppy or Sea Poppy the plants, of European origin, grow in any garden soil in a sunny place. While many species are biennial, all can be treated as annuals. Sow outdoors in September or early April, or under glass in March for hardening off later. *G. corniculatum* has lobed leaves and solitary flowers of bright red with a blackspot at the base of each petal. *G. flavum* is the yellow Horned Poppy of which the flowers are succeeded by long, horn-like seed pods. It has a form bearing orange-red flowers.

18 in. Spacing 12 in. July–September. H.A.

Godetia. Named in honour of C. H. Godet, a Swiss botanist, this is one of the most useful of garden annuals. There are a number of species some of which have been used to secure the various garden types now available. These include *G. amoena* with flowers varying in colour from deep pink to white and *G. bottae*, lilac-pink with white centre.

G. grandiflora (or *Whitneyi*) is also known as *Oenothera whitneyi*. This forms a bushy plant about 12 in high and is one of the parents of the well known dwarf Single varieties. Among the best of these, all 9–12 in, are 'Crimson Glow', crimson-scarlet; 'Duchess of Albany', white; 'Thunderbolt', crimson and 'Wild Rose', pale rose-pink.

Good single intermediate varieties, 9–12 in high, include: 'Firelight', crimson, white centre; 'Kelvedon Glory', salmon-orange; and 'Sybil Sherwood', salmon, pink-edged white.

The dwarf double or azalea flowered sorts make excellent bedding plants 12–15 in high, and include double 'Kelvedon Glory', 'Mauve Queen', 'Sweetheart', salmon-pink; and double 'Sybil Sherwood'. The tall doubles vary from 2–2½ ft, specially good being 'Cherry Red', mauve and various shades of pink. 'Lavender Gem' is single-flowered, growing about 2½ ft.

Seed can be sown outdoors in autumn for very early flowering, or in April. Give the plants plenty of room to develop, otherwise they will become weak and spindly. Take out the growing points if side shoots do not develop in the seedlings. Godetias can also be grown successfully in pots in the greenhouse.

If the taller varieties are grown in exposed positions it will be helpful to provide supports in the form of bushy sticks.

9 in–2½ ft. Spacing 6–15 in. June–October. H.A.

Gomphrena. This is the name once applied to the plant known as the amaranth, but whereas the latter is cultivated for its ornamental foliage, gomphrenas are of value for their 'everlasting' flowers. This plant flourishes in ordinary good soil and a sunny position.

Seed should be sown under glass in March, the seedlings being hardened off in the usual way for planting outdoors in early April. *G. globosa* forms ball-shaped, clover-like heads, made up of coloured bracts between which the true flowers are hidden. The colours vary including red, violet, pink and white. It has several forms such as aurea, yellow; rubra, red; and striata, with striped or speckled flower heads.

12–18 in.   Spacing 9–12 in.   July–October.   T.A.

Marigold Red Brocade

Grammanthes. The title comes from two Greek words *gramina* and *anthos* because of a marking like a letter, at the base of each petal which is why it is sometimes known as the Letter flower. Of South African origin, *G. gentianoides* has attractive little flowers ranging in colour from white to yellow and orange. It is useful for border edgings, the rock garden and for using in hanging baskets.

4–6 in. Spacing 6 in. July–October. H.H.A.

Gratiola. A native of the United States, the name is of uncertain origin. This low growing plant likes damp soil and is at its best in partially shaded situations, being quite at home on the surrounds of a pool or the lower parts of a bank. Sow seed shallowly in April where the plants are to flower and thin out the seedlings early.

G. aurea has golden-yellow flowers and lance-shaped foliage which is inclined to be sticky.

6–7 in. Spacing 6 in. June–September. H.A.

Gypsophila. Often known as the Chalk plant or Cloud plant the origin of its proper name is 'lime or chalk loving', indicating the type of soil required. Like the perennial species, the annuals are of light, graceful appearance, ideal for cutting. They should be sown in their flowering quarters in the open ground. A September sowing in a sheltered place will provide an early show, while additional seed sown in March and April, will prolong the display. In exposed or cold areas, the autumn sowings will benefit by being protected with cloches during rough weather. *G. elegans* from Asia Minor, has small, lance-shaped leaves and slender branching stems decorated with small white flowers. It has several forms having carmine, pink or purple flowers.

G. muralis is dwarf growing, rarely exceeding 6 or 7 in and therefore useful for the rock garden where its pink flowers are quite ornamental.

18 in. Spacing 9–12 in. June–October. H.A.

Hebenstreitia. This name commemorates a Professor of Medicine at Leipzig University. Of South African origin, it likes good soil and plenty of sun. Sow the seed in spring in a temperature of 65–70°F and gradually harden off the seedlings for outdoor planting at the end of May.

H. comosa is a strong grower with small white or pale yellow flowers spotted orange red. These are produced in spikes and emit a pleasing fragrance in the evenings.

There are a few other annuals species and a number of perennials in this family.

18 in.   Spacing 9–12 in.   June–September.   H.H.A.

Hedysarum. This European plant is sometimes known as the French Honeysuckle, its Latin title literally meaning Sweet Broom. Seed should be sown in unexposed positions either in late March or September, since the plants usually survive normal winter weather. Good soil and sun encourage best results.

H. coronarium has pale green pinnate leaves covered with soft hairs and dense spikes of deep red fragrant, vetch-like flowers. There is a white form although this is less attractive.

3½ ft.   Spacing 2 ft.   August–October.   H.H.A. or T.P.

Helenium. The perennial species are valued for the herbaceous border but there are a few annuals of merit. Sometimes known as Sneezewort, the name comes from the Greek *helenion*, a plant said to have some connection with Helen of Troy.

Useful plants for the border or less prominent places they grow in almost all soils and like the sun. Sow seed where the plants are to flower. Germination is sometimes slow. *H. tenuifolium* from the United States, has narrow leaves and forms shapely, bushy plants well supplied with bright yellow daisy-like flowers.

18 in.   Spacing 12 in.   July–September.   H.A.

Helianthus. Translated into English, this name means Sunflower, by which title the plant is best known. Apart from its decorative qualities the sunflower is a plant of economic value. Oil is obtained from the seed which is also useful for poultry feeding and is sometimes eaten by human beings, while the leaves have been used for fodder.

Mostly of North American origin, there are several types of annual sunflowers, which grow well in good garden soils. Seed can be sown in early April where the plants are to flower, covering to a depth of ½ in. It can also be sown under glass, the seedlings being hardened off and planted outdoors in May. Such plants will flower earlier.

H. annuus is the common garden Sunflower varying in height from 5–10 ft, which makes it useful for screening although plants need to be placed with discretion. The sturdy stems are clothed with rough pointed leaves terminating in very large yellow dark centred flowers, sometimes 10–12 in diameter. Often smaller flowers are produced lower down the stem. Seedsmen now offer variants of *H. annuus* producing paler or deeper coloured flowers, while some have smaller or double flowers. Among these varieties are *H. annuus Fl.Pl.*, the double form 6–9 ft, 'Giant Red', chestnut-red, 6 ft, 'Citrinus', primrose, 6–8 ft, 'Suttons Red', yellow with central red band, 6 ft.

Hybridists have now raised a number of small-seeded varieties some of which are now offered in seedsmen's catalogues. Apart from their flowering qualities the seed is useful for bird and poultry feeding. They include: 'Mars', yellow, dark centre; 'Pole Star', large yellow; and 'Southern Cross', another even larger yellow flowering variety.

H. argophyllus is known as the silver-leaved Sunflower, the whole plant being covered with a silvery down. The golden yellow flowers have a brownish centre. *H. debilis* (*cucumerifolius*) is of dwarf bushy habit and is sometimes known as the cucumber-leaved sunflower, the solitary yellow blooms being about 3 in diameter. It has several forms including those with yellow, and red and chestnut-brown tipped orange, flowers.

H. petiolaris from California has smaller leaves and is sometimes

Marigold Single French

known as the Prairie Sunflower. The medium-sized flowers are bright yellow with a central boss of brown.

3–10 ft.   Spacing 2–3 ft.   July–October.   H.A.

Helichrysum. This name comes from two Greek words meaning sun and gold, obviously referring to the main colouring of the flowers. This is a very large family of plants widely distributed in many parts of the world. The species and varieties grown in Britain are valued for their everlasting qualities and are frequently known as Strawflowers, being used extensively as dried flowers in bouquets and for winter decoration.

They prefer rich loamy soil and a sunny situation and always look well in the flower garden. Seed can be sown directly into flowering positions but to ensure the later flowers do not suffer weather damage, especially if they are needed for drying, sowings should be made under glass in March. Space the plants well to avoid attacks of mildew which might otherwise occur in a damp season.

H. bracteatum is the most grown species, having rounded heads of stiff incurved golden orange bracts giving a double appearance. From this species have developed types with larger heads. These are usually grouped under the sub-heading of Monstrosum and are available in many separate colours.

2–3 ft.   Spacing 10–12 in.   July–September.   H.H.A.

Heliophila. Meaning 'to love the sun'. This is an indication that this plant needs a sunny spot. Natives of South Africa, they provide a splendid display in groups in the border, while they look well grown in containers especially if 3 or 4 are grown in each 5 in pot.

H. leptophylla produces racemes of four-petalled, bright blue flowers each having a white eye. *H. linearifolia* is slightly taller with clear blue flowers.

9–12 in.   Spacing 9 in.   July–September.   H.H.A.

Heliotropium. (Heliotrope) This word comes from the Greek, meaning turning to the sun. A native of Peru and similar regions, this is strictly speaking a perennial plant but is frequently treated as an annual with the common name of Cherry Pie. Its marvellous scent and general appearance well qualifies the plant for inclusion in the annual border. The plants like a light, rich soil in a sunny sheltered position. Seed should be sown under glass in February and March, the seedlings being moved to small pots when they are growing well.

They should be ready for their outdoor positions at the end of May, while they make charming pot plants for summer and autumn flowering. Water sparingly until they are growing well and pinch the side shoots to encourage bushiness.

H. arborescens is also known as *H. peruvianum*, bears violet-purple flowers in clusters at the tops of the stems and is particularly well scented. From this species have come a number of named varieties, noteworthy being 'Madam Bruant', violet with white eye, while many seedsmen offer mixed hybrids.

1–2 ft.   Spacing 12–15 in.   June–September.   H.H.A.

Helipterum. In the Greek this title means sun and feather or wing, probably referring to the main colour and the feathery scales or plumed pappus. Chiefly natives of Australia and South Africa, this is a plant producing graceful everlasting flowers, often included among subjects known as Immortelles. The flowers are useful for a garden show and for drying purposes. Sow under glass for planting out in May or seeds can be sown outdoors in late April, covering them with ¼ in or soil.

They flourish in ordinary garden soil and like the sun. The flowers close at night when the papery heads still remain attractive, but in sunshine the petals expand. For drying, they should be cut before the central disc is prominent. *H. manglesii* is also listed as *Rhodanthe manglesii* and produces good sized, dainty rose pink flowers. There are also deeper pink and white forms. *H. roseum (acroclinium)* is excellent in the garden and when used for drying. It has single and double forms mostly in shades of pink and white.

12–18 in.   Spacing 6–9 in.   July–September.   H.A.

Hesperis. This name literally means evening, given because of the pleasant scent the flowers emit in the evening. Although most species are perennial one at least, is an annual, which however, is tender and needs a warm sheltered spot and fairly rich soil on the light side.

H. tristis from Southern Europe has small dark almost brownish purple flowers which are sweetly scented from the late afternoon onwards.

1–1½ ft.   Spacing 9–12 in.   July–September.   T.A.

Hibiscus. Coming chiefly from Africa and India, the name originally having been used for the Mallow, this subject is known as Rose Mallow. The best known species are of a shrubby, perennial nature. There are, however, a few species of annual duration. Some of the perennials too, are grown as annuals. Many of the hibiscus have a somewhat untidy habit of growth so that they should be placed with care, although the flowers of all are striking. They like good, fertile, well drained soil.

H. manihot although a perennial, is often treated as an half-hardy annual, its large open yellow flowers being conspicuously marked with crimson purple.

H. trionum (africanus) is a true annual. Sometimes known as Flower of the Hour, its large cup or funnel-shaped, creamy yellow flowers are freely produced. A form known as *Major*, is of darker colour with deep violet markings at the base of petals. It usually spills its seeds freely so that once in the garden, fresh seedlings appear each year.

1½–2 ft.   Spacing 15–18 in.   July–September.   H.A.

Hordeum. This is the Latin name for the long used cereal barley. Now that floral decoration has become an art, all kinds of material are being used including the ornamental grasses.

H. jubatum is the Squirrel Tail grass producing nodding feathery spikes of shining green which change to brown.

12–20 in.   Spacing 6 in.   June–September.   H.A.

Humulus. This title is a reference to the plant's natural habit of trailing on the ground but it is usually supported and treated as a climber. Native of China and Japan, sowings can be made outdoors in May but are best made under glass in April, the young plants being moved to the garden at the end of May. This subject is excellent for forming a quick annual screen or can be used for providing height at the back of the border.

H. scandens (japonicus) is best known as the Japanese or annual hop. It is a fast grower most useful in town gardens. An abundance of green foliage is produced, while in the form known as variegatus, the leaves are handsomely marked with silvery-white.

8–9 ft.   Spacing 1½–2 ft.   All summer.   H.H.A.

Hunnemannia. Named in honour of John Hunneman an English botanist of the nineteenth century. A native of Mexico it has several common names such as Mexican Tulip Poppy, Golden Cup, and Santa Barbara poppy.

It likes light, well drained soil in a warm, sunny situation. Sow the seeds under glass in March and the plants can be kept in the greenhouse as pot plants but are best outdoors. *H. fumariaefolia* (like fumitory) has ferny foliage making a bushy plant with long stemmed yellow, poppy-like flowers which are useful for cutting. There are a few forms of this species, one being semi-double.

18–20 in. Spacing 12 in. July–October. H.H.A.

Iberis. Many species of this annual are natives of Iberia, the old name for Spain hence the botanical title. Generally known as candytuft, they are most popular plants in the garden, useful in beds, borders and the rock garden, while they are quite valuable for cutting. The wide range of colours ensures they are in demand whenever a showy display is needed. While they are not particular about soil, one containing humus matter will encourage good results. Give the plants plenty of room to develop properly, which will also lessen the possibility of mildew. Perfectly hardy, these plants can be raised from a September sowing, when they usually come through the winter unscathed and flower early. Spring sowings can be made from March to May. Seedlings do not transplant well so thin sowing is advisable. *I. amara* is known as the Rocket Candytuft; an erect grower with fragrant white flowers. At first these are in cluster form, but lengthen to a spike. It has thickish leaves and is often known and used by florists as the hyacinth-flowered candytuft. It has a dwarf form known as pygmea.

I. umbellata is the candytuft most commonly seen in gardens and sometimes referred to as the Globe candytuft. The flowers are scentless, but the colour range is wide, many named varieties in carmine, crimson, rose, lilac and white being offered by seedsmen as well as mixtures of colours.

6–15 in. Spacing 6–8 in. June–October. H.A.

Impatiens. Often known as Balsams, these plants have long been popular in the greenhouse and garden. The name impatiens is from the Latin referring to the fact that when the ripe seed pods are touched, they immediately burst scattering the seed in all directions and do not wait until gathered as do most other subjects. They also have the common name of Touch Me Not for obvious reasons.

Seed can be sown in open ground when danger of frost is past or in the cool greenhouse from early March onwards. Useful as greenhouse plants, they grow better when under glass than in the open ground.

Ionopsidium. This name comes from two Greek words meaning

103

violet-like and the subject is sometimes known as Violet Cress or Diamond Flower. A native of Portugal and other tropical places, it is a delightful little plant for sowing from April to June on the rock garden or front of the border where it is to flower. It forms neat specimens useful at the base of taller growing subjects. It freely produces itself from self-sown seedlings and looks well in pots or pans.

I. acaule has tiny, four-petalled lilac or white flowers often tinged violet. It matures quickly flowering within 8 or 9 weeks from time of sowing.

4 in. Spacing 4–5 in. June–October. H.A.

I. balsamina, the garden balsam, makes a splendid display as a bedding or border plant. The stems are supple so must be handled with care. Usually offered as a mixture, it is possible to obtain separate colours in shades of red, pink, lilac, violet and purple.

I. camelliaeflora is the Camellia flowered balsam with large double blooms again in mixture and separate colours.

I. holstii is really a perennial pot plant, but is often treated as an annual having brilliant scarlet flowers up to 2 in in diameter.

I. roylei (*grandulefera*) is a useful species which can sometimes be found wild in Britain. A strong grower often reaching 3 or 4 ft high, it has flowers varying from purplish-rose to white. Sow directly in the open. *I. noli-tangere* grows in moist positions being suitable for the wild garden and having pale·yellow flowers spotted red. Can be sown straight outdoors.

The well known *I. sultanii* is a greenhouse perennial often known as Busy Lizzie.

1½ ft. Spacing 12 in. July–October. T.A. and H.A.

Ipomoea. Although the meaning of this name is convolvulus or Bindweed-like, it must not be assumed that the subject is liable to become a nuisance as are some plants often known as convolvulus. This is a very large family from tropical and temperate parts of the world, many being perennials, but some are splendid annuals. The large showy flowers usually make a fleeting appearance but this habit is made up for by the freedom with which they are produced.

There has always been some confusion regarding the naming of some of the species. A few are still referred to as convolvulus, others are known under the names of calonyction or Quamoclit. Another and more appropriate name is Morning Glory.

A good but not over rich soil is needed. Root conditions which are too good lead to much stem and leaf growth but fewer flowers. Some species need to be sown in the greenhouse while a few can be sown outdoors in sheltered places.

I. hederacea, has more or less ivy-shaped foliage and medium sized funnel-shaped flowers of deep blue with red shading at the edges. It has several different coloured varieties.

I. nil is similar to hederacea having forms with blue, violet, rose and white flowers. Seedsmen offer a number of varieties which also appear to belong to the group. These include 'Scarlet O'Hara' which is wine-red and quite attractive.

I. purpurea has been cultivated for centuries and is ideal for covering fences, trellis work or for rambling over unsightly objects. Seed is available in varieties of separate colours although it is more often catalogued as mixed. All the foregoing species can be sown in sheltered positions outdoors.

I. quamoclit is sometimes known as the Cypress Vine and really needs to be grown in the greenhouse or outdoors in a particularly warm, well drained situation. It has finely divided ornamental foliage and small scarlet tubular flowers.

I. rubro-caerulea (tricolor) is a most lovely annual climber, its large sky-blue trumpet-shaped flowers showing up well against the large heart-shaped leaves. There appear to be several slightly different forms and Heavenly Blue with clear sky-blue flowers is particularly good.

I. versicolor. See *Mina lobata*.

6 ft. Spacing 18 in. July–September. T.A.

Jasione. This name is of uncertain origin and even the common European name of Sheeps-bit is obscure in meaning. It is useful for edging or filling in spaces in the rock garden, having no special cultural needs.

Sow in open ground in April, or in September to stand the winter, which it will on all but extremely rare occasions.

J. jankae has clusters of mid-blue flowers looking like little pincushions. *J. montana* is rather larger growing with pale blue flowers.

12 in. Spacing 4–5 in. July–September. H.A.

Kaulfussia. See *charieis*.

Kickxia. Although still sometimes listed under linaria to which they are very similar, this is an ancient name for a small group of annual creeping herbs. Natives of Asia and Europe including Britain, the stems are clothed with alternate, sometimes opposite, leaves and solitary axillary flowers.

While not very showy, these plants are useful for covering bare spaces in the rockery while they have been used successfully on dry walls. They like fairly light soil and either partial shade or full sun. Seed should be sown in flowering positions in April, germination being sometimes a little slow.

K. elantine has dark green, hairy, heart-shaped leaves and tiny yellow

Petunia Single mixed

flowers of which the lip is marked purple. *K. spuria* has bigger and rounder foliage with darker purple markings.

Creeping. Spacing 6 in. July–October. H.A.

Klugia. This is the commemorative name of a small group of tender annuals from Mexico and India, first introduced to Britain last century. These somewhat rare plants are attractive seen in the cool greenhouse where seed should be sown in early spring in a temperature of around 70°F or, for winter flowering, sow in June or July. For the latter purpose keep the plants under cool conditions to begin with so that they do not make too much growth before October. Once flower buds are seen, more warmth can be given. When the seedlings can be handled easily prick them off into 3 in pots then gradually move to the 5 in size. Since they have rather succulent stems they must not be kept in a dry atmosphere.

K. notoniana has oval leaves with a sharp point, the blue flowers having a white lip. *K. zeylanica* is rather smaller with slight differences on the shape of the flowers.

10–12 in. Pots. July–October. T.A.

Kochia. Named after a German botanist W. D. J. Koch (1771–1849), this is an excellent foliage plant. There are several dozen species but only one is in general cultivation. It grows in ordinary garden soil and likes a sunny, open but not exposed, position. It also makes a charming pot plant in the cool greenhouse or conservatory.

Sow seed in light soil in the greenhouse during March and April. In a temperature of 60–65°F germination occurs within a week. Sown in the cold frame growth will be slower. Transplant the seedlings into boxes or pots and harden off for putting outdoors in late May. Plants being grown in pots will benefit from liquid feeds from July onwards.

K. scoparia has several common names including Summer Cypress and Mock Cypress. It forms an erect but compact bush of finely cut tender-looking foliage. The flowers in the leaf axils are quite small and inconspicuous. In the early autumn the foliage gradually changes colour until it assumes lively rich autumn tints. There are two forms of *K. scoparia*. The one known as *Childsii* retains its fresh green colouring for the whole season but *tricophylla*, the best form of all, takes on most wonderful autumn hues finally becoming a lustrous russet red causing it to be known as the Burning Bush.

2–3 ft. Spacing 1½ ft. Summer and Autumn. H.H.A.

Lagenaria. This title comes from the Latin meaning a bottle, in reference to the shape of some of the fruit, which are often known as ornamental gourds. This subject has been cultivated for centuries and is useful as a climber for covering unsightly trellis work and fences during the summer months. Plants should be raised in the same way as melons or cucumbers. Sow the seed $\frac{1}{2}$ in deep in small pots in April. Gradually harden off the plants for putting outdoors in late May, choosing warm sunny sheltered positions. The fruits, useful for indoor decoration during winter, should not be cut until ripe. This can be determined by making sure the fruit stem is hard and beginning to crack, and becoming brown, and the skin of the fruit also being very firm. Hang up the cut fruit to dry for 2 or 3 weeks. If they are then given a coat of copal varnish they will remain in good condition for months.

L. siceraria (vulgaris) is the main species grown in Britain and seed is usually available in mixture. It is also possible to obtain seed of separate shapes such as bottle, dipper, siphon, horn, gooseberry, spoon and turban as well as those having a wart-like skin. There are too, fruits of which the skin is ribbed or is half green and half orange yellow.

In Africa, Calabash pipes are made from the outer shells of the fruits, while elsewhere they have been utilised for making musical instruments.

Climber. Spacing 3–5 ft. July–October. H.H.A.

Lagurus. This is an ornamental grass often known as Hare's-tail grass, which is actually the meaning of the Latin title. It flourishes in ordinary garden soil which is not liable to remain wet. Sow seed in April and May where the plants are to mature. Sowings may also be made in pots in the cold frame at the end of August. Such action will result in earlier and probably better flowering the following summer. This is a useful subject to include in floral arrangements and bouquets. For this purpose the spikes can be lightly dried. This means cutting them as soon as the flowers open and placing them in an airy, cool, dry place, preferably hanging them up in small bunches.

L. ovata produces soft woolly plumes usually $\frac{1}{2}$ in long.

1–1$\frac{1}{2}$ ft. Spacing 6–7 in. July–October. H.A.

Larkspur. See *delphinium*.

Lathyrus. This is an ancient Greek name for a family of many species best known of which is *L. odoratus* usually referred to as the Sweet Pea. There are a number of other species which are nothing like so attractive as the modern varieties of *L. odoratus*. These include:

L. albus (*pannonicus*) forming clusters of small white flowers on climbing stems. There is also a pink form.

L. sativus is the Chickling Vetch from Southern Europe and Asia. The whitish flowers are shaded or marked blue. Its form known as azurea has attractive, clear blue flowers from July to September, making it quite a pleasing plant to include at the back of an annual border.

Phacelia campanularia

L. tingitanus is known as the Tangier Pea. It has small purple and scarlet flowers and is useful for growing in little clumps at the back of the border or similar positions.

L. odoratus was introduced to this country from Sicily in 1699. In that year a monk, Franciscus Cupani, sent seed to a Dr. Uvedale of Enfield. The plants raised produced small undistinguished flowers of a magenta shade about the size of those of a culinary pea. Little development seems to have occurred for almost 100 years when it is recorded that a number of other good colours were in cultivation. It was not until toward the end of last century that any serious attempt was made to improve the sweet pea. Breeders in Britain and the United States were most active but it was Henry Eckford a grower of Wem, Shropshire, who by careful selection and hybridising eliminated the plants weak points but improved the size, texture and colour of the sweet pea. Above all he retained the marvellous scent which today is the main reason of this flower being so much sought after.

The next major development was the discovery early in this century of the frilled flowered type. Previously all of Eckford's varieties were known as grandifloras or large flowered. The standards were plain, often hooded. The first frilled or waved form was discovered by Silas Cole of Althorp Park Gardens, Northampton. The waved type he named after his employer Countess Spencer which is why the frilled varieties are usually referred to as Spencer Sweet Peas. The passing of time has yielded very many improvements and developments brought about by growers in various parts of the world.

The Spencers remain favourites and new varieties are introduced annually in almost every colour tone, except yellow. Some good creams are available but as yet, nothing approaching a real yellow. Any list of varieties is likely to become out of date within a few years but specialist growers offer a wide range of named sorts. It pays to look through catalogues annually in order to keep up to date.

Apart from the Spencers many other sections are available. These include the following groups:

Early Multiflora with 5–8 well spaced flowers on a stem. Excellent for greenhouse culture as well as outdoor display.

Galaxy multiflora are exceptionally vigorous with a long flowering period. These regularly produce 5–7 strong stems. They are available in many named sorts.

California semi-dwarf. Flowers grow about 3 ft high with strong growth. The flower spikes are ideal for cutting.

Knee-Hi is the name of another semi-dwarf type, also growing about 3 ft.

Of the really dwarf sorts there is Early Bijou growing 12-15 in high and making spreading bushes.

Little Sweetheart forms neat compact bushes 8-12 in high, according to soil and situation. These are useful for pots and window boxes.

The so-called Old Fashioned sweet pea is now available again. It is very fragrant, although the flowers themselves are quite small compared with other modern types and not waved. Their perfume makes up for any disadvantage in this respect.

The sweet pea has a long flowering period, growth is free and luxuriant above and below ground level. Following nature, we find that seeds ripen and are shed in the late summer and autumn, therefore this is the natural time to sow, a supposition borne out by experience, for better results follow autumn sowing. Secondly, the sweet pea is much hardier than many suppose and will withstand the frosts we get in this country, nine seasons out of ten, without any protection. 100% hardy if given the protection of a cold frame or cloches, provided always the glass is not placed over the plants except during very frosty or very wet weather in the winter, any attempt at coddling or forcing is resented at all stages of growth.

Left to its own devices, without crowding or hampering, the plants grow luxuriantly. Therefore, over-crowding at all stages is wrong. The plants like sunlight, so choose a position in the garden that is open and sunny all day long. Apart from the fact that sweet peas do not like too much chalk, they will grow well in almost any kind of soil to be found in this country. The root system is naturally deep and wide-searching, so for best results we must provide conditions whereby those roots can develop in a normal manner by digging deeply or trenching, although many growers do not move the soil beyond one spit deep.

To sustain a free, luxuriant haulm growth, and freedom of flowering over a long period, feeding agents should be given liberally, and of such a nature that they release their nutriment gradually over a lengthy period. Animal manure or other organic agents should be used in preference to chemical fertilisers. Bone Meal is excellent, but should always be used in conjunction with animal manure. Where the latter is unobtainable, use good compost and bone meal with a top dressing of wood ash in spring.

As far as seed sowing is concerned, in drier parts of the country, seed is sown directly into flowering positions in early October. Other growers wait until March before sowing in the open. Perhaps the best way is to sow in pots or trays in early February or March in the cool greenhouse or cold frame, gradually hardening off the plants for putting outdoors from the end of March onwards.

For exhibition purposes, sow in the autumn in pots in a cold frame, plunging the pots to their rims in fibre, soil or old ashes. Some growers transplant the seedlings singly to small pots in mid winter, but keep the pots in the frame. In autumn or early winter, the site is deeply trenched 2–3 ft deep, mixing in a liberal dressing of well decayed animal manure and bone meal, keeping the manure well mixed throughout, except the top 9 in but bone meal is mixed throughout the entire trench. Good compost can take the place of manure if this is unobtainable. Most soils benefit from a dressing of lime scattered on the surface in winter. From mid to the end of March the seedlings are transplanted, using a trowel or dibber, not less than 6 in apart, in single or double rows. Some growers plant out without disturbing the ball of soil round the roots, others prefer to gently shake off the old potting soil.

Support the plants immediately with small twigs. Later give them permanent supports, usually most prefer 8–9 ft bamboo canes, fastened to a light framework. When plants are about a foot high, pruning or restriction of growth commences. Each plant has all growths nipped out or cut away excepting the strongest basal side growth, and this is trained up the cane by means of wire split rings or bass ties. Thus we see that a plant which has been encouraged to develop its root system to the utmost underground has its growth above the ground pruned and restricted very considerably.

Lavatera. Named in honour of the brothers Lavater who were botanists and physicians in the eighteenth century, this is a family of showy plants of differing habits of growth. Coming from Mediterranean regions, Australia, and Southern Europe the annual species are deservedly popular. Seeds can be sown in April where the plants are to flower during summer and autumn but if sown in a sheltered position in September, they produce even finer plants. This subject does not transplant well and likes sun and a draught-free site.

L. trimestris and its forms are the best for general culture and sometimes appear in catalogues as *L. rosea* or *L. splendens,* but these are not the specific names. The plants produce in profusion, rose pink, trumpet-shaped flowers up to 4 in diameter and form erect bushy plants with pale green, deep toothed leaves, which sometimes are almost round and at others are angled. It has white and pink forms, one selection known as Sunset, producing especially fine shining, rich rose-pink flowers.

L. mauritanica is sometimes available. This is rather shorter growing having deeply lobed leaves with woolly hairs, the violet flowers being marked purple.

2–4 ft. Spacing 1½–2 ft. July–September. H.A.

Layia. This group of Californian plants owe their name to G. T. Lay, a nineteenth century naturalist. A subject of easy culture it looks well in groups near the front of the border where seed can be sown in April in its flowering position. It has the common name of Tidy Tips because the daisy-like flowers usually have petals tipped with white.

L. elegans is the most widely grown. It forms branching plants and large yellow flowers, well edged white. The grey green, soft, hairy leaves often well divided, emit a pleasant scent. It has a form known as alba with pure white flowers.

L. glandulosa has narrow pointed leaves, the white flowers often being tinged rose. Excellent for cutting.

L. platyglossa has broad yellow petals, well edged with white. Provided the plants are in a sunny position they continue to flower longer than the other species.

10–12 in. Spacing 9 in. July–September. H.A.

Leptosiphon. See *gilia.*

Leptosyne. In some ways this is somewhat like coreopsis, in fact, some species are sometimes catalogued as coreopsis and both belong to the same genus. The name itself comes from the Greek meaning slenderness in reference to the slender flower stems. Natives of California and Mexico, seed can be sown in warmth in March under glass or in the open ground from early May, thinning them well.

L. douglasii (*californica*) has upright foliage with bright lemon-yellow daisy-like flowers.

L. maritima, often listed as a coreopsis, is known as the Sea Dahlia and produces large golden yellow flowers like single dahlias.

L. stillmannii is probably the best species of neat habit. It has large lemon-yellow blooms but the double form is, however, much better and probably the best of all leptosynes. Known as 'Golden Rosette', it is a first class cut flower.

1½–2½ ft. Spacing 8–9 in. July–October. H.A.

Limnanthes. A native of California and other parts of the U.S.A., this is a very hardy little plant of which the name means 'marsh flower' indicating its liking for moist conditions. A low spreading subject, it creates a real show although having such simple needs. Excellent for border edgings, the rock garden and attractive to bees, this subject is useful for supplying early greenhouse colour. Sow where the plants are to bloom and by sowing at different times, flowers can be had from May to September. For the earliest a September sowing is necessary.

These plants thrive almost anywhere, which is surprising in view of their origin. In fact, they seem to do just as well in dull wet seasons as in dry, warm years.

L. alba has saucer-shaped, white flowers and finely cut foliage. *L. douglasii* has scented salver-shaped flowers of yellow, shading to white at the tips of the petals. It is sometimes known as Butter and Eggs and also Meadow Foam. A larger form known as *grandiflora*, is occasionally available.

This subject seeds itself very freely and sometimes it is necessary to get rid of some of these self-sown plants.

6–8 in. Spacing 6 in. May–September. H.A.

Limonium. This is the name of the plants often known as annual statice and of which the proper name actually means 'from the meadow', an allusion to the fact that this plant, also known as Sea Lavender, is found growing wild in Mediterranean areas as well as in other regions. Cultivation is of the simplest. Sow in open ground in April or May or for early flowering, under glass in March for hardening off. For even earlier flowers, sow in September keeping the plants in a cool greenhouse during the winter. The blooms are prized as everlastings for winter decoration, while they are widely grown for marketing. When dried, the papery flowers keep their colour and generally last well indoors.

L. bonduelli throws up branching stems of bright yellow flowers and is particularly good for greenhouse decoration and for pots.

L. sinuatum (*sinuata*) has much cut foliage and heads of paper-like blue flowers. From this species has come many separate colours so that, apart from the mixed 'Art Shades', it is sometimes possible to obtain seeds of individual shades such as lavender, white, orange, pink and buff.

L. suworowii is of quite different habit and has a rosette of lance-shaped leaves from the centre of which arise long, dense cylindrical spikes of rose-pink flowers. Sometimes known as Pink Pokers, they are valued by florists.

18–24 in.   Spacing 12 in.   July–October.   H.H.A.

Linaria. The foliage of some species of linaria resembles linum or flax the root of both names being linon. There are scores of species native of widely separated parts of the world. Having the common name of Toadflax, these charming plants are of simple culture and very suitable for the border and rock garden, some succeeding on

Rudbeckia Sputnik

dry walls or in the crevices of crazy paving. A well drained soil and an open sunny situation is to their liking. They are also attractive grown in pots or pans.

Seed can be sown outdoors during March and April and in sheltered positions. September sowing leads to bushier, earlier flowering plants. Seed can also be sown in pots in September keeping them in the cold frame to begin with, afterwards moving the plants to a cold or very cool greenhouse for the winter. Water sparingly and ventilate freely. If the faded flowers are cut off before seed forms, fresh shoots will break out from the base.

The flowers resemble miniature antirrhinums and they are useful for cutting, lasting a long time in water.

L. alpina is the alpine Toadflax and is often of biennial habit. Once plants become established in the rock garden or walls they seed themselves freely, new plants reappearing annually. The colour is violet blue, the lower lip being marked orange. There are several forms in which pink or orange colouring predominates.

L. biportita makes bushy little plants with narrow bluish-green leaves and violet purple flowers marked orange. This too has several forms.

L. broussonnettii is rich, orange-spotted black being excellent for the rock garden. *L. cymbalaria*, is known as Kenilworth Ivy or Mother of Thousands. Strictly speaking a perennial, it grows so freely that it is worth treating as an annual. A splendid subject for semi-shady moist positions its trailing growths are covered with lilac flowers having a yellow throat while there are pink and white forms.

L. heterophylla is lemon yellow. Its variety splendens takes in crimson violet and bronzy shades.

L. maroccana is one of the best, having slender branching stems, narrow pointed leaves and spikes of violet purple flowers. A strain known as Excelsior produces a wonderful mixture of bright colours and it is possible to obtain separate named varieties to colour.

L. reticulata has strong stems bearing attractive crimson purple flowers, splashed deep yellow and covered with a network of purplish veins. *L. tristis* forms hardy plants with narrow leaves, the yellow flowers being marked with crimson or bronze. In spite of its name, it blooms in the daytime and not at night.

6–12 in.   Spacing 5–8 in.   June–October.   H.A.

Lindheimera. A little known North American subject of obscure origin, seed should be sown under glass in March in a temperature of 60–65°F, the seedlings being pricked out and hardened off in the usual manner. It is helpful to take out the growing points to encourage a bushy habit. A fairly rich, light soil in a sunny situation should be given.

L. texana from North America has heads of attractive golden-yellow flowers, an inch or so in diameter and not unlike those of ornamental tobacco with oval, rather pointed leaves.

2½–3 ft. Spacing 2 ft. June–October. H.H.A.

Linum. Natives of North America and parts of Asia, the Latin name simply means flax, by which title the plants are commonly known. This subject gives a generous return for very little trouble. Seed should be sown in succession from late March to June, where the plants are to bloom. Most useful for the border or wild garden, they show colour over a long period.

L. grandiflorum, the Scarlet flax, is of erect branching habit and there are forms having deep red, rose and white blooms.

L. usitatissimum is the annual flax with pale blue flowers. It is from this species that linseed oil is extracted and the fibres provide commercial flax. In the garden its continuous flowering will give much pleasure.

1–2 ft. Spacing 9–10 in. June–September. H.A.

Loasa. This somewhat odd group of annuals sometimes known as Chilian Nettles are more curious than beautiful. Even the origin of their name is uncertain although some authorities believe it is derived from the name of a Spanish naturalist. They are not fastidious about growing conditions but seem to do best in an open sunny situation and a medium soil. Seed is sown in April where the plants are to flower.

The leaves are fairly ornamental with well cut edges *but* they are densely covered with sharp, stinging hairs so that it is advisable to wear gloves when handling the plants. Handled carelessly, the irritation may last for days.

L. tricolor has bright yellow flowers patterned red and white. *L. urens* (*hispida*) which literally means stinging, has prettily cut leaves but penetrating stinging hairs. The light yellow flowers are marked white and green.

L. vulcanica is white, the centre of the flowers being marked yellow, red and white.

15–18 in. Spacing 10–12 in. July–September. H.A.

Lobelia. Named in honour of Dr Matthew Lobel or L'obel, a botanist and physician to James I, this is a large genus containing perennial, biennial and annual species. Some of the most widely grown varieties are actually perennials but are almost always treated as annuals in Great Britain. They are among the most widely grown plants for summer bedding, either as edging subjects or for use in large groups. They are first class for window boxes and hanging baskets—especially the trailing varieties—while many make excellent pot plants.

Sowings should be made in boxes or pots from February onwards in a temperature of 60°F, sowing very thinly and shallowly. Prick out the seedlings when they can be handled and if they do not show signs of becoming bushy, pinch out the growing points. For a very early flowering, seed should be sown in trays or pots in late September wintering the plants in a cool greenhouse. *L. erinus* from South Africa, is a variable species from which have been derived many excellent garden varieties. Its main colouring is light blue or violet, with white or yellow throat markings.

Among the best varieties which have come from *L. erinus* are 'Blue Gown', rich deep blue; 'Blue Stone', clear blue; 'Cambridge Blue', light blue; 'Crystal Palace', blue flowers and bronze foliage; 'Mrs. Clibran', deep blue with white eye and *kermesina oculata*, rose crimson with white eye; and 'White Lady'.

There are also varieties with gold or bronze foliage. A few doubles can sometimes be had, but do not breed true from seed.

L. erinus pendula is sometimes known as the spreading or trailing lobelia and is available in various named strains including: 'Gracilis', deep blue; 'Miranda', rosy-crimson; white eye; 'Sapphire', deep blue, white eye; and *speciosa*, bright blue.

Compact varieties.

4–6 in. Spacing 6 in. June–September. H.H.A.

Trailing varieties.

8–12 in. Spacing 9 in. June–September. H.H.A.

Lonas is an uncommon annual from the Mediterranean regions. The origin of the name is uncertain. It likes a light, fairly rich soil in an open sunny situation. Seed should be sown in March in a temperature of 60–65°F, the seedlings being hardened off for planting outside in May and June.

L. inodora (*annua*) forms a branching plant suitable for the border. Its bright yellow flowers, produced in clusters, are valuable for cutting. They are useful for drying for use in winter as everlastings, treating them the same as helechrysum.

12 in.   Spacing 10–12 in.   July–October.   H.H.A.

Lopezia. The name of this Mexican plant commemorates Juan Lopez, a Spanish botanist. This is a charming subject which can be sown in its flowering positions or can be germinated under glass in March and April. It likes moderately light soil and flourishes in the sun although it also grows well in partial shade.

L. coronata forms neat bushy plants with reddish stems clothed in glossy green pointed leaves. The pinkish-red flowers are followed by

Rhodanthe roseum

small seed pods carried horizontally.

12 in.   Spacing 6–7 in.   August–September.   H.A.

Lophospermum. See *Maurandya*.

Lotus. The origin of this name is uncertain although said by some authorities to be after the Lotus of Theophrastus. The majority of the species, which come from Asia, Europe and North America, are perennials but two are annuals worthy of mention. Both grow in good soil without any problems. Seed should be sown in early April where the plants are to flower. Sometimes known as Birds-foot Trefoil, the foliage is well divided as is all species of the leguminosae.

L. ornithopioides has diamond-shaped leaves and yellow pea-like flowers. *L. tetragonolobus (purpureus)* has pale green leaves divided into three and purple-red flowers followed by seed pods which are out of proportion to the flowers looking rather like a square cucumber up to 4 or 5 in long. This is a peculiar rather than attractive subject.

6 in.   Spacing 10–12 in.   July–September.   H.A.

Love Lies Bleeding. See *Amaranthus*.

Luffa. This is a tender annual from the tropics producing curious sponge-like fruits. Often known as loofahs, they are members of the cucumber family and climb by means of their well branched tendrils. Seed should be sown ½ in deep under glass, in February or March in a temperature of 65–70°F. Prick off the seedlings singly into pots and lower the temperature but maintain a fairly humid atmosphere. Hand pollination of the female flowers is needed. These flowers can be recognised by the miniature fruits behind the petals. The pollen from the male flowers is transferred to the stigmas by means of a camel hair or similar brush. When the fruits begin to swell, give weak liquid manure at 7–10 day intervals.

Eventually the fruits should be taken from the plants and placed in a sunny position in the greenhouse. When the skin begins to crack, it should be carefully stripped off and the seeds emptied out.

L. acutangula is the Dish Cloth Gourd, growing up to 10 ft high, the fruits or loofahs measuring 10–12 in long.

L. cylindrica has stems 10–12 ft long, the yellow flowers being followed by cylindrical fruits from 15–24 in long. This is the loofah of commerce.

10–12 ft.   Spacing 6 ft.   July–September.   H.H.A.

Lupinus. While the perennial lupins are so well known, the annual species have been unjustly neglected. The family name comes from the Latin *lupus*, so given because it was once widely believed that lupins impoverished the soil. This is far from true. In fact, lupin seed is sometimes sown for the purpose of digging in the seedlings to provide green manure. There are species originating in Europe, and various parts of the United States as well as Mexico. Seed is sown in spring where the plants are to flower. Thin out the seedlings so that the remaining plants have room to develop fully. Sowings can also be made in September, in sheltered positions to secure earlier blooms.

L. *albus* with white flowers is often used as a fodder plant but is useful in the less prominent parts of the garden.

2–3 ft.

L. *densiflorus* is a branching plant, having yellow, white or rose pink flowers according to variety.

1½–2 ft.

L. *hartwegii* is particularly good, since it forms an erect plant, the type itself having blue flowers marked white on the standards. Named sorts include *albus*, white; 'Coelestinus', sky blue; *roseus*, rose-pink; and *rubra*, deep red. All grow 1½–3 ft although recently some dwarfer forms have been introduced.

L. *hirsutissimus* from California has spikes of large reddish-purple flowers. The leaves are hairy and often irritate a tender skin.

1½–2½ ft.

L. *hirsutus* is the well known annual blue lupin, often used as an agricultural plant, the blue flowers on slender spikes being tipped white. This too, has varieties of different colours.

2–3 ft.

L. *luteus*, often known as the yellow lupin. This is also used as a fodder plant. One pleasing thing about these for the garden, is that the flowers are deliciously scented.

1½–2 ft.

L. *mutabilis* from South America is a taller growing species of bushy habit, having spikes of sweet scented white flowers, the standards being flushed lavender and marked with yellow. It has several named varieties including *Cruickshanksii* which is blue, shaded yellow with pinkish markings on the wings. This too has several forms with blue, pink and white, and blue and white flowers.

4–4½ ft.

L. nanus is a dwarf grower with scented blue and white flowers while there are varieties having white, white and rose, and violet and white flowers. Useful for bedding and edging.

9–14 in.

L. pilosum, a robust annual has hairy leaves and rose pink flowers, of which the standards are marked red.

3–4 ft.

L. pubescens, a native of Mexico and Central America has soft, green, well divided leaves covered with downy hairs. It has spikes of violet-blue flowers marked white on the standards. A free flowering species, it has given rise to many hybrids, a number of which are sometimes offered in seedsmen's catalogues.

2–3 ft.

L. subscarnosus (*texensis*). An attractive dwarf species succeeding in all soils. The rich blue flowers are often marked or spotted white or yellow.

9–12 in.

L. sulpheureus is a strong grower with soft foliage and long spikes of sulphur yellow flowers. Apt to become untidy.

2½–3 ft.

A particularly fine newer strain is that known as Dwarf Russell Minarette, which is earlier flowering than the perennial Russells and blooms the first year from an early sowing.

1½ ft.

Dwarfer still, is the annual 'Pixie Delight' which comes in a mixture of bright colours.

6 in–5 ft.   Spacing 6 in–3 ft.   June–October.   H.A.

Lychnis coeli-rosa. See *agrostemma*.

Lychnis oculata. See *viscaria*.

Lythrum. While the perennial forms are well known, the annual lythrum, which name means 'dark blood', referring to the colour of the flowers, is rarely cultivated. It grows in ordinary garden soil and can be sown in April where the plants are to flower.

L. hyssopifolium is a narrow hyssop-leaved plant, the whorls of deep purple-red flowers being borne at the top of the stem.

15 in.   Spacing 4–5 in.   July–September.   H.A.

Madia. A Chilean name for a plant originating in West America as well as Chile. A useful oil is obtained from the leaves which if rubbed send out an odour rather like that of turpentine. This subject has the unusual habit of flowering best in semi-shade for when in full sun, the petals close. Seed should be sown in April where the plants are to bloom.

M. elegans is the American species having daisy-like flowers similar to coreopsis, the yellow petals having a brownish red zone at the base.

M. sativa from Chile, is smaller and less attractive although it is said to be the best for its oil.

18–30 in. Spacing 12–18 in. July–September. H.A.

Malcolmia. Best known as Virginian Stock, the Latin name commemorating W. Malcolm, a London nurseryman of the eighteenth century. This is a very popular and showy annual which will grow and seed itself almost anywhere. Useful for edgings, the rock garden and odd patches, it is liked by children for its ability to brighten odd corners. Sow in spring, or in well drained positions in September.

M. maritima is usually available as a mixture of showy colours although separate varieties in crimson, white, pink, carmine and much less common yellow, are sometimes available.

6–8 in. Spacing 3–4 in. May–October. H.A.

Malope. An ancient name for members of the Mallow family, said to refer to the softness of the leaves of some species. These old fashioned plants are natives of North Africa and other Mediterranean regions. They like a fairly rich soil and when this is so, they flower continuously throughout the summer months. Sow in the open ground during April and May.

M. trifida (*grandiflora*) has large rosy purple flowers and it is from this species that other colours have been developed. These include deep rose, pink, crimson and white.

2–3 ft. Spacing 12–15 in. July–October. H.A.

Malva. Sometimes known as the curled Mallow, this name comes from the soothing properties of the leaves which were once used for garnishing.

Sow in spring in the open ground preferably in a sunny position. *M. crispa* makes a tallish bush, its broad leaves being elegantly curled. The small white flowers are inconspicuous.

4–5 ft. Spacing 2 ft. July–September. H.A.

Martynia. Named in honour of a Cambridge botanist of the eighteenth century, this is now often classified under the genera proboscidea.

They are rather curious plants suitable for the cool greenhouse, although occasionally they can be found growing well in a warm, sunny position outdoors. Because of the peculiar shaped fruits produced, this subject is sometimes known as the Unicorn plant or Elephant's Trunk. Sow in small pots in the warm greenhouse during March and April, potting on the plants until they reach the 6 in size where they can look impressive when in fruit. Although usually grown for ornamental purposes, the fruits can be used in pickles in the same way as gherkins, if gathered while young.

18–20 in. Spacing 15–18 in. June–September. Fruits. H.H.A.

Matricaria. This title comes from the Latin word meaning matrix, mater or mother, possibly because of the supposed soothing qualities of some of the plants. There is considerable doubt regarding the grouping of some of the species and a number of them are to be found listed under *Chrysanthemum parthenium* or placed with pyrethrums. The single forms are sometimes known as Mayweeds although some of them are far superior to the wild plant often known by that name. Useful bedding subjects, seed should be sown under glass in March, the seedlings being placed in flowering positions in May.

M. inodora, so named because its foliage, is almost free from the normal pungent scent of the matricarias. The white flowers are semi-double

M. parthenoides will sometimes persist throughout the winter. The freely produced flowers are small and usually single. It has several double flowering forms which are valued for summer bedding including *eximia fl. pl.* which in turn, has two forms 'Silver Ball' and 'Golden Ball'.

M. multiflora is a half-hardy subject from South Africa. Its deeply cut leaves are strong smelling so the plants should not be handled more than necessary.

9–15 in. Spacing 9–10 in. July–October. H.A.

Matthiola. Named after P. A. Matthioli, an Italian doctor and botanist, this family of plants takes in a number of well known subjects, many of which are simply known as Stocks. Some are natives of Europe, others come from South Africa and Mediterranean regions. Without at least a few Stocks most gardens would be the poorer. In some cases, the modern hybrids are better than the species from which they have been derived. It is somewhat difficult to separate some of the biennial stocks from those that are truly annual, since some of the biennials are grown as annuals. It is possible by selecting varieties from several sections to have flowering plants throughout most of the year.

The well known Brompton Stocks are biennials. The true annual stocks can conveniently be grouped as summer, autumn or winter flowering. Undoubtedly the summer flowering, so called ten week strains, are the most popular of all. They are so named because they can be brought into flower within ten weeks of time of sowing which is usually in March. Sown under glass then, the young plants will have grown sufficiently strong to have been hardened off for planting outdoors in May,

M. incana var. annua is the official title of all the ten week stocks, the plants having long greyish foliage. There are several strains which, by the proper cultural procedure, will result in all the plants producing double flowers, an aim sought by most gardeners. There is, of course, no serious drawback in having a few single flowering plants in a bed, although many gardeners strongly dislike such a happening.

Nemesia Large Flowered hybrids

The strain known as 100% Double Park is one of the most grown at the present time. This is available in separate colours as well as a mixture, all growing 15–18 in high. The procedure for securing double forms is as follows: raise the seedlings in warmth under glass as usual, and when they are about ½ in high, move them to a cool temperature of 40–45°F for 2 or 3 days. It will then be found that some have dark green leaves, whilst others are a much lighter green. Transplant the latter, which are the doubles.

The strain known as Giant Perfection Ten Week produces flowering spikes 18–24 in long.

Of more recent development is the Trysomic Seven Week strain which will mature in seven weeks from time of sowing, being available in a mixture of colours and these are one of the earliest flowering types. They first produce a central spike followed by numerous side branches. If, at the four leaf seedling stage, the weaker plants are discarded the remaining specimens may be expected to produce double flowers.

Nicotiana Sensation mixed

The Giant Excelsior Column stocks do not branch, but form single stems 2–2½ ft long. The individual flowers are large, making a first class spike for decorative work. Various named varieties to colour, as well as good mixtures are offered by all the leading seedsmen.

A shorter, earlier flowering form of the Giant Excelsior type is also available under the heading of Double Early Cascade. As with the Excelsior strain, each plant produces a single spike closely set with large florets.

Beauty of Nice sometimes classed as Winter Beauty or Mammoth Stock forms strong branching, pyramidal growth up to 2 ft high. They are all a little later than the Ten Week type. Very free flowering, the spikes are long lasting making this strain most suitable for both bedding and cut flower purposes. The original 'Beauty of Nice' variety with flush pink blooms has long been popular in Britain, France and other countries. From this variety quite a large number of named sorts in separate colours have been developed. They include rose, carmine, crimson, white, creamy-yellow and rosy-lilac.

M. sinuata is a vigorous branching plant having rather wavy-edged leaves and it is from this species and others, that the East Lothian or Intermediate stocks have been developed. Growing 15–18 in high these are available in a number of separate colours.

To provide flowers during the summer, seed should be sown in gentle heat in January and February treating them in the same way as the Ten Week strain. They can also be sown a little later to provide early autumn blooms. It is, however, quite customary to sow them in August in prepared beds outdoors in sheltered positions treating them as biennials. The seedlings are moved to their flowering positions in late September where, under congenial conditions, they will bloom in early spring.

Brompton Stocks are of course true biennials, seed being sown in the open in July, the plants being put in their final positions in September for flowering the following summer. To help avoid winter losses, it is advisable to sow not later than mid July and to transplant the seedlings at least twice. This encourages the production of a good fibrous root system and strong stocky growth.

1–3 ft. Spacing 6–10 in. June–October. H.H.A.

Matthiola bicornis is the Night Scented stock and is worth growing because of the delicious perfume the lilac or purplish flowers emit when they open in the evening. This fragrance more than makes up for the rather sad picture the plants present when the flowers are closed and rather drooping appearance in the day time. Some gardeners have overcome this drawback to some extent by mixing seed with that of Virginian Stock (*Malcolmia*), the latter providing a generous colourful display during daylight hours. Seed can be sown from early April onwards where the plants are to flower.

1–1½ ft. Spacing 6–8 in. June–September. H.A.

Maurandya (*maurandia*) This little known group of Mexican climbing plants was named after Professor Maurandy of Carthagena. They are really tender perennials but almost always grown as half-hardy annuals. Sow in early spring remembering that germination is often slow. Prick off directly into small pots giving more room as growth develops. Light rich soil suits them and some kind of support should be provided. Once established they climb well and flower freely. While they are best in a cool greenhouse they will succeed outdoors in a warm, sheltered, well drained position.

M. barclayana has small leaves and gloxinia-like purple flowers. There are several forms with white or deep pink blooms and seedsmen often offer them in mixture.

M. erubescens is of hairy appearance with rosy-red flowers. *M. lophospermum* (*scandens*) has heart-shaped leaves and rosy red or purplish flowers.

Climbers. Spacing 18 in. July–October. H.H.A.

Mentzelia. Named after Christian Mentzel, a botanist who lived in the seventeenth century, this subject is best known as *Bartonia aurea*. A useful annual for pots, it should not be overlooked in the summer border. It likes a sunny position and light soil and produces many golden yellow blooms with prominent stamens, the entire flower glistening in the sunshine.

M. lindleyii (*Bartonia aurea*) has golden yellow flowers up to 2½ in in diameter. Sow in the open in April or in the cool greenhouse in March for planting out later.

15–18 in. Spacing 9–10 in. July–October. H.A.

Mesembryanthemum. The meaning of this name which is 'Mid day flower', is a clear indication that the flowers are open and at their best in sunshine and good light. They are ideal plants for any sunny situation, always creating attention when the blooms are open.

Sow in warmth in March and April for moving to flowering positions in late May onwards, or sow directly into good open sunny positions in May. Too much moisture can lead to much foliage rather than flowers.

M. criniflorum (*dorotheanus*) is known as the Livingstone Daisy. A native of South Africa it is a low growing, spreading plant which covers itself with large daisy-like flowers in very bright colours taking in pink, salmon, apricot, crimson, yellow and white. It makes a carpet of colour.

M. cystallinum (*cryophytum*) is the Ice Plant, and is cultivated for its curious foliage rather than its insignificant white flowers. This foliage is covered with glistening minute sacs containing moisture giving a most striking effect.

M. pyropaeum (*tricolor*) which literally means 'fiery eyed' is another pretty, low growing species which likes hot dry positions. The freely produced flowers having a dark eye are in shades of rosy red, pink and white.

3–4 in. Spacing 6 in. July–October. H.H.A.

Mimulus. The title of this plant comes from the Latin *mimic* referring to the supposed resemblance of the flowers to a mask or monkey's face. It is sometimes known as Monkey Flower or Monkey Musk. Apart from the perennial varieties there are a number of annuals, or perennials grown as half-hardy annuals. They are excellent pot plants as well as being showy outdoors. They like sun and moisture although often they grow well in partial shade. The seed is very tiny indeed and it is best to sow it on the surface of fine soil and either leave it uncovered or simply pressed in with the fingers.

M. brevipes from California, is the yellow Monkey Flower. *M. cardinalis* produces scarlet, long lipped flowers. It shows several forms and seed is sometimes available in mixture.

M. cupreus is often grown as a perennial, its coppery red blooms being most attractive. The mixed strains taking in red and scarlet are often treated as half-hardy annuals, and those known as 'Red Emperor' and 'Whitecroft Scarlet' are specially good.

M. fremontii is known as the Pink Monkey Flower, its large flowers varying in colour from rose to crimson with deeper throat. *M. luteus* from Chile is also grown as an annual. The flowers are yellow blotched crimson, but it is the mixed strain such as Queen's Prize that is strikingly beautiful.

10–12 in. Spacing 9–12 in. July–October. H.H.A.

Mirabilis. The name of this South American plant means 'to be admired'. Various common titles have been given to the subject including Marvel of Peru and Four O' Clock. The latter name arises from the fact that the flowers only open in late afternoon or on cloudy days.

Sow the seed under glass in March and move the seedlings outdoors in late May or June.

M. jalapa has funnel-shaped flowers up to 2 in long in shades of red, pink, yellow, white and striped varieties. *M. longiflora* has longer narrower tubular flowers which are nicely scented in the evenings. Colours include white, rose and violet.

2–3 ft. Spacing 12–15 in. July–September. H.H.A.

Moldavica. See *Dracocephalum.*

Morning Glory. See *Ipomoea.*

Namaqualand Daisy. See *Venidium.*

Nasturtium. See *Tropaeolum.*

Medicago. This family of annuals and perennials is native of various parts of Europe and Asia. The annual forms are worth growing as curiosities rather than being plants of any special value. Seed should be sown in March or April where they are to flower, thinning out the seedlings early.

M. echinus is known as Calvary Clover. Coming from Southern France, it has pale green leaves and clustered heads of clover-like bright yellow flowers. Each leaf is marked with a deep red spot while the coiled spiny fruits which follow, resemble a crown of thorns. As a novelty it can be grown for indoor decoration, keeping the pots in full light on the window sill. Three plants in a 5 in pot will create a pleasing display.

M. prostrata has somewhat trailing stems and is useful for the rock garden where its yellow flowers show up well in either sun or shade.

6 in. Spacing 6–7 in. June–September. H.A.

Mina lobata. Sometimes catalogued as *Ipomoea versicolor* and *Quamoclit lobata*, this name indicates that the plant is a member of the convolvulus family. A native of Mexico, this is a beautiful, free-flowering climbing plant which succeeds under glass and in warm, sheltered positions outdoors. The finely divided pinnate foliage is quite handsome, while the tubular scarlet flower buds open to a yellowish shade passing to cream. There is also a white flowering variety. Both are worth a place where room can be found for them.

Sow seed in pots in warmth in March or April, potting on the seedlings according to growth. Plants for outdoors should be gradually hardened off for putting out in late May or June.

8–12 ft. Spacing 15 in. July–September. T.A.

Molucella. A half-hardy annual, native of both Europe and some Mediterranean regions, this subject has during recent years become very popular among flower arrangers. One of the species is reckoned to be a native of Molucca and at one time this whole family was known under the name of Molucca. This unusual subject is useful for the border and the wild garden, preferring a light well drained position.

Seed should be sown under glass in March, and after about three weeks the seedlings should be pricked out and grown on in a lower temperature for planting outdoors in May.

M. laevis is the best known species and popularly referred to as Bells of Ireland or the Shell Flower. It has rounded coarsely crenated leaves on long stalks, each small white or pale pink fragrant flower being set inside a very large, shell-like pale green calyx, which is prettily veined. Seed of this can be sown in May in flowering positions but the flowers will be later.

M. spinosa is much less common. It is taller than *M. laevis*, the calyx being spiny and therefore less convenient to handle.

2½–3½ ft. Spacing 9–15 in. July–September. H.H.A.

Momordica. This subject is grown for its fruit and foliage rather than its flowers. Mostly natives of tropical Africa and Asia, the name is derived from the Latin, meaning to bite, the seeds having the appearance of having been bitten. Useful and unusual climbers for the cool greenhouse, they will also succeed in warm sheltered positions outdoors where they look well clambering over trellis-work, fences and walls. They like fairly rich soil and plenty of sun. For fruiting outdoors, sow in March and the young plants need to be hardened off before being placed in the garden.

M. balsamina is sometimes known as the Balsam Apple. The yellow flowers have a dark centre and are followed by orange, egg-shaped fruit.

M. charantia is the Balsam Pear with pointed orange fruit, while there are several other good species.

5–7 ft. Spacing 12–18 in. July–September. H.H.A.

Nemesia. This name was first used centuries ago for some other plant, but has now become firmly attached to the plant we know as nemesia. A native of South Africa it can now be classed among the most popular of half-hardy bedding plants, while in pots it gives a pleasing display. Seeds are usually sown in warmth in March for outdoor planting in late May. The fluffy seed as received in packets, has a mildewed appearance, although the actual seed is inside the 'fluff'. Never subject the seedlings to a lot of heat and if they show signs of becoming thin and straggly, pinch out the growing points. Seed sown outdoors in late May will usually flower in late summer and autumn.

A sowing can also be made in the cold frame at the end of August, the seedlings being potted and taken into the cool or warm greenhouse in November in order to secure flowering plants from January onwards. Sowings in September and October provide spring flowering plants. Although there are a number of species few are offered by seedsmen.

N. lilacina has narrow leaves and well branched sprays of lilac flowers marked yellow.

N. strumosa varies in colour taking in shades of yellow, purplish-blue and white. It is from this species that the modern garden varieties have descended. Almost all of these hybrids are superior to the parent both in colour and habit.

Present day varieties are usually grouped as compacta strains which are of dwarf bushy habit and the larger flowered, taller sorts, sometimes identified as Suttonii varieties. These Suttonii varieties are useful for border work, the flowers usually having long stems which are valuable for cutting. In addition to the mixture, separate colours are available including those with blotched flowers.

Nemesia compacta or *compacta nana* varieties, form neat little plants, ideal for edging and bedding, all flowering profusely. Among named varieties are the following: 'Blue Gem', brilliant blue; 'Fire King', scarlet; 'Orange Prince', deep orange; and 'Triumph' mixed.

Compacta varieties.

6–9 in. Spacing 6 in. June–September. H.H.A.

Suttonii type.

12–15 in. Spacing 8–10 in. July–September. H.H.A.

Nemophila. The translation of this name is grove loving, indicating the places where these plants are often to be found growing in North America. They are useful for edging purposes, the rock garden, or for grouping in the border. Easy to grow, they seem to prefer cool, moist soils. They do not transplant well and seed should be sown where the plants are to bloom. It is usual to sow in spring for summer and autumn flowering, although in well drained unexposed places, sowings can be made in September for very early flowering. September sowings in pots also provide interesting spring flowering plants for the cool greenhouse.

Sometimes known as the Californian Bluebell, this description gives an idea of the colour and shape of the flowers.

N. aurita is of trailing habit with deep violet flowers up to an inch in diameter.

N. insignis is probably the best known species. It has the common name of Baby Blue Eyes, the large gentian-blue flowers usually having a white centre. Of more or less prostrate habit, it is showy for the front of the border. It has a larger form known as grandiflora and another, alba, has white flowers.

N. menziesii appears to be similar if not the same as *N. insignis*, as does *N. modistii*. There may be slight botanical differences of little interest to the gardener, such as the colour of the stamens, although occasionally forms with very dark petals or a white edging appear.

6–7 in. Spacing 8–9 in. June–September. H.A.

Nicandra. This name is commemorative of Nicander, a very ancient botanist and writer. A native of South America and sometimes known as the Apple of Peru, seeds should be sown in April where the plants are to grow or plants can be raised under glass earlier. Give them room to develop and discard seedlings which are in any way poor.

N. physaloides forms a strong growing, spreading plant with pale blue flowers, followed by berries contained in calyces. These curving fruits are sometimes cut for winter decoration. There is an equally strong growing form known as *violacea*, the white flowers shading to violet.

3 ft. Spacing 2 ft. June–September. H.A.

Nicotiana. This plant was named after Jean Nicot, a French Ambassador, who, in the sixteenth century, is said to have presented tobacco to the Courts of Portugal and France.

Although perennials in their native habitats of North or South America, in Britain, they are always treated as half-hardy annuals and are not to be confused with smoking tobacco.

The foliage is quite attractive but it is for their fragrance that the ornamental nicotianas or tobacco plants are grown. All like a deep rich soil and good treatment will be reflected in the results obtained. The majority of the species emit their pleasing fragrance during the evenings or dull days, the flowers remaining closed in the daytime. Recently however, a form has been introduced which opens its flowers throughout the day.

N. alata has white flowers tinged violet on the outside. Its large flowered form, grandiflora, is usually listed as *N. affinis* and has highly scented flowers, which only open fully in the evenings.

There are forms with scarlet and crimson flowers, Crimson Bedder being most reliable.

N. hybrida, 'Daylight' is dwarfer than the other species but has the distinct advantage that its white flowers remain open during the day.

Sweet Sultan

It can also be obtained in a form known as White Bedder and as a mixed strain under the name Sensation.

N. sanderae was raised in Britain and is a hybrid of distinction with carmine rose flowers. The *sanderae* hybrids are a real acquisition with flowers in shades of crimson, carmine, mauve and white.

N. suaveolens is another species with very sweet smelling flowers. Coming from Australia, it has proved first class as a pot plant.

Several other hybrids have recently been introduced notably 'Lime Green', an unusual and attractive shade of greenish-yellow, and 'Idol', the deep red flowers opening in daytime. It is valuable for pot work.

2–2½ ft. Spacing 12–15 in. July–September. H.H.A.

Nigella. This deservedly popular annual owes its name to the Latin *niger*, meaning black, a reference to the colour of the seeds. Well known as Love-in-a-Mist and Devil-in-a-Bush, it has dainty light green filigree foliage which surrounds the saucer-shaped flowers which are followed by the 'fruits' containing the black seeds.

Spring sowings can be made from March onwards but the largest and earliest flowers are obtained by sowing in the open ground in September, selecting good soil and a sunny position. *N. damascena* is a species from South Eastern Europe with blue, purple and white flowers. It is its forms, and notably 'Miss Jekyll', rich Cambridge blue, which are now usually grown. There is also a white form but it is the strain known as 'Persian Jewels' which is most popular. It takes in a new range of colours including pink, carmine, mauve, lavender and purple.

N. hispanica has deep blue flowers with red stamens and responds well if the seed pods are cut and dried for winter decoration.

N. sativa is less common. It has greenish-yellow flowers sometimes shaded blue. The aromatic seed is said to be useful in cooking because of the fennel scent which has caused them to be known as the Fennel Flower.

1½–2 ft. Spacing 9 in. June–September. H.A.

Nolana. Sometimes known as the Chilean Bellflower which indicates the country of origin, the Latin name comes from *nola* meaning little bell, referring to the shape of the flowers. So long as the position is sunny, this subject will grow in quite poor, sandy soil. Splendid for edging and in borders they look well trailing in pots or hanging baskets, the convolvulus-like flowers being a most beautiful blue varying in depth and tone, according to variety. Sow in flowering position in spring or under glass in pots in September.

N. atriplicifolia (syn. N. grandiflora and **N. paradoxa)** is an attractive plant with spreading stems and oval, pointed leaves, the blue flowers having white and yellow zones.

N. lanceolata is one of the best, its sky blue flowers having showy white and yellow centres.

N. prostrata is distinguished by its spatula shaped leaves and white throated blue flowers, which are $\frac{3}{4}$ in in diameter.

6 in. Spacing 12–15 in. July–September. Trailing. H.H.A.

Nycterinia. See *Zaluzianskya*.

Oenothera. The origin of this name is somewhat obscure. The word literally means wine chase, a possible allusion to the once held belief that if certain plants were sprinkled with wine they were likely to assist in taming wild animals! It is the delightful scent of many of the species in this large family of perennial and biennial plants, some of which are best treated as annuals, which makes them so valuable in the border. They are natives of temperate parts of North and South America.

Sow under glass in March for transplanting outdoors in a warm sunny position in May. These plants have the common name of Evening Primroses and well deserve increased cultivation.

O. acaulis is really a trailing plant, the stems rarely growing more than 6 in long. It has finely cut foliage and lilac white flowers which shade to pink with age. It has a good yellow form. *O. biennis* is the popular large, scented yellow species. *O. bistorta* has golden-yellow flowers, usually marked with a black spot. These remain open in the daytime whereas some species close.

O. odorata is larger growing with good sized, yellow-scented flowers which become tinged with red as they grow old. It has a form with paler yellow flowers.

O. trichocalyx has bluish green, long, cut leaves and large white flowers produced singly and remaining open during daytime.

6–30 in. Spacing 6–8 in. July–September. H.A.

Omphalodes. The word means naval like hence the common name of Venus's Navelwort. Sometimes catalogued as *Cynoglossum linifolium* it comes from Portugal and Spain. Sow seed in flowering positions in spring or September.

O. linifolia bears creamy white flowers in forget-me-not-like fashion

136

and has greyish green foliage. An excellent subject for the rock garden or front of the border, looking best in groups.

9–12 in. Spacing 6–10 in. July–October. H.A.

Onoseris. This subject is a native of Central and Southern America the meaning of the name being obscure. Although a little known half-hardy plant, it can be quite attractive as a summer bedding subject. A light, fairly rich soil, and a sunny sheltered situation should be selected. The seed needs sowing in March in a temperature around 65°F, the seedlings being pricked out and potted on in the usual way. Place them in the cold frame in April, for hardening off and planting out in May or early June.

O. reflexa has erect branching stems with cut-edged, pointed leaves, which with the stems, are covered with woolly hairs. The large fragrant yellow flowers are valuable for cutting. In exposed positions the stems may need supports to keep them upright.

2 ft. Spacing 6 in. July–September. T.A.

Orthocarpus. This name comes from the Greek and means straight

Statice sinuata (limonium)

fruit referring to the shape of the seed pods. It is a charming plant for the annual border and grows well in good soil in a sunny position looking specially fine in groups. Sow the seed in April where the plants are to flower.

O. lithospermoides from California has erect stems and oblong, hairy leaves, with dense spikes of yellow flowers, the lower lip being inflated so that it looks like a sac. *O. purpurescens* has finely divided leaves and a stocky spike of crimson-purple flowers marked with shades of red, yellow and white.

12 in. Spacing 6 in. July–September. H.A.

Osteospermum. See *Tripteris*.

Oxalis. Often known as Wood Sorrels most of the species are perennial but a few are treated as annuals. The name comes from the Greek *oxis* meaning sharp or acid in reference to the taste of the leaves. This is a large family of plants consisting of both perennials and annuals, coming chiefly from South America, and South Africa, although a few are natives of Britain. They have attractive foliage and are effective in the rock garden or for growing on walls, between crazy paving and for border edges. Quite hardy, they grow well in soil which does not dry out and prefer semi-shade to full sunlight. Sow in open ground in April in a light, well drained position or they can be grown in pots or pans. In common with the perennial species, those treated as annuals have leaves sensitive to light and fold in the evening as do the flowers in dull weather.

O. corniculata (*O. stricta* or *O. lutea*). A native of Britain, this has heart-shaped divided leaves and yellow, funnel-shaped flowers. A form known as *var. atropurpurea* has crimson-purple foliage. *O. valdiviensis* (*valdiviana*) comes from Chile. It has bright green leaves divided into three and thick clusters of bright yellow flowers of which the inside is striped brown.

Seeds are freely produced and it usually becomes necessary to ruthlessly thin out the seedlings to keep this subject from becoming invasive.

6 in. Spacing 6–7 in. July–September. H.A.

Palana (*Palava*). Named in honour of a Spanish botanist of the nineteenth century. Natives of Chile and Peru, these are half-hardy annuals useful for pots in the cool greenhouse or for growing in little groups in beds and borders. Sow under glass in March, plants for outdoor culture being gradually hardened off for planting at the end of May. They like a moderately rich soil and a sunny situation. While they look well as cut flowers, they do not last long in water.

P. dissecta (flexuosa) makes bushy little plants with finely cut foliage, the branching stems producing attractive, lavender-lilac, mallow-like flowers with white centres and red stamens. *P. rhombifolia* has diamond-shaped leaves and fine terminal clusters of rose-coloured flowers. 9–12 in. Spacing 5–6 in. June–September. H.H.A.

Papaver. This is the correct name for the plants usually referred to as Poppies, although the origin of the title is a little uncertain. It may come from the Greek *papa*, meaning thick-milk, a reference to the white juice emitted from the stems when cut.

Poppies have universal appeal and there are so many species and varieties in general cultivation. Although the blooms do not last as long as many other subjects, they are produced in great profusion helping to make up for the limited display of individual flowers.

Annual papavers like a fairly light, well drained sunny situation. Sow seed shallowly in early April, thinning out the seedlings early. They look best when placed in groups. Any necessary transplants should be done when the plants are small, The flowers are seen at their best when growing in the garden. If they are used for cutting, they must be gathered while they are young. In fact, as soon as the colour can be seen between the expanding sepals.

P. nudicaule, the Iceland Poppy, is really a short lived perennial, but is very often treated as an annual. This species has deep yellow or orange flowers, but it is strains that have been developed from *P. nudicaule* that are so valuable. These include 'Kelmscott Giant', 'Coonara' and 'Gartref' which together, take in a wide colour range including some with a picotee edge.

P. pavoninum from Turkestan, is known as the Peacock Poppy, having bright scarlet flowers with a dark base to each petal. *P. rhoeas* is the Corn poppy, a native of Britain and other European countries. It has scarlet blooms and from it have been developed many useful strains. Among these, are the Shirley poppies, bred by the Rev. Wilkes of Shirley about 85 years ago and having a tremendously wide colour range. A reliable double strain is known as 'Ryburgh hybrids'. Several other types have also been introduced including the Begonia flowered, Ranunculus flowered and the Pompom type.

139

P. somniferum, meaning sleep-inducing, is the Opium poppy from Greece. It has much cut grey-green leaves. The single flowers are normally white, often shaded reddish-purple. A number of varieties have come from this species, both single and double flowers, including the carnation-flowered and paeony-flowered types.

15–20 in. Spacing 12 in. July–September. H.A.

Pennisetum. The two Latin words making up this name mean feather bristle indicating the feathery plumes produced by this ornamental grass. Most species of this African subject are perennials but a few are usually grown as annuals. They like sandy soil in a sheltered, well drained position, or start in boxes in April for planting out later.

P. villosum (*longistylum*) has graceful flower heads useful for cutting and mixing with colourful flowers or for drying for winter use.

2 ft. Spacing 15 in. July–September. H.A.

Perilla. This is the name of the plant frequently grown in North India although it also flourishes in China and Japan. Sometimes known as the Beefsteak plant, this subject is now regaining the popularity it has lost during the past 30 years. This in part at least, is due to the recently introduced strains which are much more colourful than the older which, although once much used for bedding, were of sombre appearance. It is said that in Eastern countries the seeds are crushed in order to extract perilla oil using it as a substitute for linseed oil.

Sow in the cool greenhouse in March for planting outdoors towards the end of May. These plants are ideal as dot subjects among colourful flowering annuals. *P. nankinensis* (*P. frutescens var. crispa*) has deep purple leaves with a bronzy lustre. There are several forms including *laciniata* with much cut foliage and *macrophylla* with large purplish leaves.

12–18 in. Spacing 12–18 in. Foliage plant. H.H.A.

Petunia. This name comes from a Brazilian word, *petun*, said to be connected with tobacco, a closely related genus. They are among the best of half-hardy annuals for summer display. While they prefer a warm sunny situation they will give a creditable display even in dull damp seasons.

Hardly any of the original species are now grown, the hybrids having outstripped them in every way.

Seed should be sown thinly and shallowly in warmth in March, the seedlings being pricked out when they can be handled easily.

For the best display, plants should be moved to small pots when they are an inch high but whether in pots or boxes, they will gradually harden off in the cold frame for planting outdoors about the end of May.

P. axillaris (nyctaginiflora) is noteworthy for its night scented, funnel-shaped whitish flowers. It is one of the parents of the first of the modern hybrids.

P. hybrida is of garden origin and it is from this that many of the present day named petunias have come. For convenience these hybrids have been made into separate groups. This helps in determining something of the appearance and size of a particular variety. Reference to seedsmen's catalogues will give some idea of the range of named sorts.

P. hybrida grandiflora takes in the large flowered, single types including those with ruffled flowers. It also includes double-flowering varieties very suitable for pot culture. The double multiflora varieties have frilled carnation like flowers, while the single multiflora have smaller blooms and it is these which are much used for bedding purposes. One of the reasons they are so popular is that they are so continuous flowering and seem to recover quickly after heavy rains.

P. hybrida pendula is the Balcony or Cascade petunia of spreading or trailing habit and first class for hanging baskets and window boxes. New varieties are introduced annually in an almost bewildering range of colours.

During recent years the introduction of F.1 hybrids has meant even more interest being shown in these delightfully showy plants.

Large flowered.
15–18 in. Spacing 9 in. July–September. H.H.A.
Giant Ruffled.
18–22 in. Spacing 9–10 in. July–September. H.H.A.
Small flowered.
15–20 in. Spacing 8–9 in. July–September. H.H.A.
Dwarf hybrida nana.
10–15 in. Spacing 6–9 in. July–September. H.H.A.

Phacelia. This name comes from a Greek word *phakelos* meaning a cluster or bundle, an indication of the way in which the flowers are arranged. Coming almost entirely from North America, this is a genus of plant liking a sunny position and a light well drained soil.

Seed is best sown thinly in late spring and early summer where the plants are to produce their attractive, bell-shaped flowers which are a great draw to bees.

P. campanularia is the best known species producing heads of large rich blue flowers of outstanding beauty. The oval-pointed, irregularly toothed leaves are produced on reddish stems. Apart from its use outdoors it makes a pleasing pot plant. It has a pure white form. Both have prominent yellow stamens.

P. ciliata has lavender-blue, sweet scented flowers and leaves divided into several segments.

P. congesta has pale green, ferny foliage of irregular shape and heads of small, pale blue flowers with protruding mauve stamens and white anthers. *P. parryi* has well lobed leaves and wide mouthed, deep violet flowers with white anthers.

P. tanacetifolia has much cut foliage and soft lavender flowers which attract bees. Should be grown where the soil does not dry out.

P. viscida (*eutoca*). The foliage exudes a tacky substances through its leaf hairs. The gentian blue flowers are especially attractive to bees.

P. whitlavia (*Whitlavia grandiflora*). Sometimes known as the Californian Bluebell this species has oval-toothed leaves and large clusters of purple-blue, bell-shaped flowers. This too, has sticky hairs covering the leaf surface. It has a white form as well as one in which the white petal deepens to blue at the centres.

9–24 in. Spacing 6–10 in. July–September. H.A.

Phlox. The literal interpretation of this name is flame, indicating the brilliance of the flowers. There are several dozen species in this large family of plants from North America and Siberia, although comparatively few are in cultivation, the many hybrids from the various sections being better than a lot of the species.

Phlox drummondii is named after Thomas Drummond who collected the seeds in Texas fairly early in the nineteenth century and sent supplies to Britain.

Of easy culture, seed is sown in gentle heat in March using a general soil mixture of loam, leaf mould and silver sand. Prick out the seedlings early so that they do not become starved and weak, for they rarely recover properly if this happens. They should be gradually hardened off for planting outdoors at the end of May. These plants are useful for bedding, window boxes, and pots, while they look well grown round taller, summer-flowering plants acting as a kind of ground cover.

From this species three sections have been developed, grouped according to size, all having lance-shaped leaves and terminal clusters of flowers.

P. drummondii gigantea is the largest form, the individual flowers usually being in excess of an inch in diameter, growth being more upright than the other groups. There are a number of separate named sorts but the mixture known as Art Shades takes in many beautiful colour tones, almost all having a paler centre.

P. drummondii grandiflora is the tallest growing section and because of this, the plants are liable to become untidy looking. The flowers are rather smaller than the gigantea group. Here again, good named sorts are offered by seedsmen in a delightful colour range.

P. drummondii nana compacta. Varieties in this section are the best for edging and dwarf bedding. They make compact bushy growths smothered with most showy flowers. Apart from the separate colours, the Cecily mixture is particularly colourful while the newer Twinkle Dwarf Star mixed has dainty star-like flowers carried above the foliage.

P. drummondii grandiflora.

12–18 in. Spacing 9–10 in. June September. H.H.A.

P. drummondii gigantea.

10–12 in. Spacing 8–9 in. June–September. H.H.A.

P. drummondii nana compacta.

5–6 in. Spacing 7–9 in. June–September. H.H.A.

Platystemon. This name simply means broad stamen, an allusion to the expanded filaments carrying the anthers. In some ways this Californian plant resembles an attractive meconopsis having poppy-like flowers. Sow the seed thinly in light soil in a sunny situation, at the front of the border or selected places in the rock garden.

P. californicus (leiocarpus) has the common name of Cream Cups. It forms a shapely plant producing numerous creamy yellow flowers with six spreading petals. A deeper coloured form is sometimes available. This has rather downy silvery-grey foliage.

6–9 in. Spacing 6–8 in. July–September. H.A.

Poinsettia. See *Euphorbia*.

Polygala. At one time certain species of this subject were said to increase the milk yield of cattle when the plants were eaten in pasture land. This is indicated in the name *polygala* which in Greek literally means much milk.

This is an easily grown annual for the front of the border or the rock garden. Sow in flowering positions in April and May. *P. lutea* from North America and sometimes known as Milkwort produces clusters of brilliant orange flowers over a long period.

9 in. Spacing 8–9 in. June–September. H.A.

Polygonum. Often known as Knotweed because of the many

Vinca Little Bright Eyes

jointed stems this characteristic is indicated in the name which means 'many kneed'. Some species in this fairly large family are rightly regarded as weeds. There are numerous perennial species, but a few of the annuals are worth growing. Their rather rampant growth makes some of them useful for forming screens or backgrounds to borders. Although they can be sown in the open ground in April and May, it is best to start them in gentle heat in March. Apart from liking a sunny unexposed position they have no special cultural needs.

P. arenarium is a prostrate species just a few inches high. It simply smothers itself with creamy white flowers. *P. orientale (persicaria)* is a fast growing plant sometimes known as Prince's Feather. Quite an old-fashioned subject it produces largish foliage and spikes of rather drooping panicles of flowers, 7 or 8 in long. There are less common forms with creamy flowers and one with variegated foliage.

P. persicaria is known as Lady's Thumb having narrow green leaves marked with a darker green triangle, and short spikes of pinkish green flowers.

2–3 ft. Spacing 12–15 in. July–September. H.H.A.

Poor Man's Weatherglass. See *Anagallis*.

Poppy. See *Papaver*.

Portulaca. This is an old fashioned name for the plant often known as purslane. Many of the species are grown in the kitchen garden but one or two are interesting flowering subjects. These plants do not need a rich soil and in fact will flourish in quite poor ground so long as the situation is warm and sunny and is well drained. Excellent carpeting plants, they are ideal for border edgings or rock garden, providing a display throughout the summer. While seed can be sown in early April under glass for raising plants for outdoor planting in May, it is best to sow where the plants are to flower since they do not always transplant well.

P. grandiflora from Brazil is known as the Sun plant and Rose Moss. It has fleshy leaves and wiry semi-prostrate stems which produce large flowers in a very wide range of brilliant colours. These flowers need plenty of sun if they are to keep opening fully. While it is sometimes possible to secure separate colours it is the double flowered mixed that is so very good.

6 in. Spacing 6–9 in. July–September. H.A.

Pot Marigold. See *Calendula*.

Proboscidea. See *Martynia*.

Quaking Grass. See *Briza*.

Quamoclit. See *Ipomaea*.

Reseda. When plants were used more for medicinal purposes, this subject was employed to relieve pain. The literal meaning of the name being I calm. To-day it is best known and valued as Mignonette, possessing an unique and powerful scent. Not only is this an excellent garden subject but is valuable when cultivated in pots.

Seed can be sown in open ground in April or in pots in the cool greenhouse in March, or in autumn if very early flowers are required. Handle them with care since the stems are brittle.

Some species are native to Britain. These include *R. lutea*, yellowish-green and *R. alba*, whitish, but these are of little value as garden plants. *R. odorata* with yellowish-white flowers is the most important species. Coming from North Africa, it is too well known to need description. A number of varieties have come from this species notably 'Crimson Giant', large red, 'Golden Queen', 'Golden Giant' and 'Bismarck', large spikes of red.

A group of varieties under the heading of Machet is particularly good, separate colours including yellow, copper and red.

12–15 in. Spacing 9 in. June–September. H.A.

Rhodanthe. See *Helipterum*.

Ricinus. This name is the Latin for a tick, an insect which the seed is said to resemble. A native of tropical Africa, this plant has several common names including Castor Oil Plant and Palma Christi. The bean-like seeds often prettily marked and coloured, should be sown in March ½ in deep, in a temperature around 65°F. The seedlings should be potted on and gradually hardened off before planting them outdoors in June. Germination is sometimes slow and for that reason, many gardeners soak the seed in tepid water for twenty four hours before sowing.

Some of the varieties make splendid pot plants for conservatory, greenhouse or living room decoration. Outdoors, the plants may grow quite large, so unless they are in a sheltered position, it is advisable to provide some kind of support against strong winds.

R. cummunus is really a perennial, but in Britain it is grown as an annual foliage plant, fresh seed being sown each year. This species reaches tree-like proportions in warmer countries and at various times it has been used medicinally, chiefly for the oil that is extracted from the seeds. This species is a fast grower, producing large palmate leaves and quite big spiny seed pods. It has several useful garden forms including *borboniensis arboreus*, with red stems and blue-grey leaves while *cambodgensis* has black stems and deep bronzy-red foliage. It is *gibsonii* which is specially useful. This is smaller growing, having dwarf, red metallic foliage, while *laciniatus* is a variety with light green deeply cut leaves.

3–8 ft. Spacing 2–4 ft. Summer and Autumn. H.H.A.

Ricotia. This name is thought to commemorate an obscure Italian botanist. An annual plant from the Mediterranean regions, this is a branching herb very useful for border edgings or for the wild garden.

Sow the seeds in April where the plants are to flower or, in sheltered situations, it can be sown in September. *R. lunaria* is of rather spreading habit with divided leaves and clusters of pale lilac flowers. These are followed by flat, thin, half-moon shaped seed pods.

6–9 in. Spacing 4–6 in. June–September. H.A.

Roemeria. Named in honour of J. J. Roemer, a botanist who lived in the late seventeenth century, this is a little group of plants chiefly native of the Mediterranean regions. Seed should be sown in spring in sunny positions where the soil is fairly dry.

R. violacla (hybrida) is known as the Violet Horned Poppy which can very occasionally be found growing wild in Britain but is rarely offered by seedsmen. It forms bushy plants with finely cut foliage, its violet purple flowers being 2 in or more in diameter.

R. refracta is even less easy to obtain. It has red flowers, the petals being marked maroon at the base.

12–18 in. Spacing 12 in. June–August. H.A.

Rudbeckia. Often known as coneflower, the official name commemorates Olaf Rudbeck, a Swedish botanist who lived from 1660–1740. This is an excellent family of plants from North America which are easily grown, fine for garden decoration and long lasting as cut flowers.

Sow seed under glass in March and April, hardening off the seedlings for outdoor planting towards the end of May. *R. bicolor* is very free flowering, the yellow petals being marked purplish black at the base, while the central disc is black. It has several forms including superba, with larger flowers, and semi-plena, with semi-double and fully double blooms.

147

'Kelvedon Star' has rich yellow flowers zoned mahogany, with a brownish centre. Bambi makes dwarf bushy plants with flowers of rich bronze, chestnut and gold. Tetra 'Sputnik' takes in a selection producing flowers with broad petals in colours ranging from lemon to rich gold, all with a dark central zone.

R. hirta is often known as Black Eyed Susan. Although perennial, it is usually treated as an annual. The type flower is yellow with orange shading. In cultivation many other colours have developed including bronze and crimson, all with a zoned centre, large flowered hybrids such as 'My Joy' with large golden blooms and 'Autumn Leaves' a grand mixture of lovely autumn tints. The so-called Gloriosa Daisies are available in single and double forms on long stems and in many beautiful shades.

1–2½ ft.   Spacing 1½ ft.   July–October.   H.H.A.

Sabbatia. This name honours L. Sabbati, an Italian botanist of the eighteenth century. While plants can be successfully grown in the cool greenhouse, they are quite suitable for flowering in the open ground. Sow in gentle heat in March or early April, and move to flowering positions in late May. They like a light, well drained soil.

S. capestris is free flowering, the colour being rich pink with a prominent yellow centre of stamens. *S. stellaris* has pink star-like flowers, each with a yellow eye.

9–12 in.   Spacing 6–7 in.   June–August.   H.H.A.

Ursinia hybrids

Sage. See *Salvia*.

Salpiglossis. Two Greek words meaning trumpet and tongue, give the clue to the description of this South American plant since they refer to both the shape of the flower and the leaf.

These half-hardy annuals make splendid pot plants and are sometimes seen to advantage in the pot plant classes at flower shows. Sowings made in August will produce flowering plants the following May. Other sowings early in the year, will provide colour from July onwards. Although they can be made, sowings directly into the open ground in late May, are risky but outdoor specimens can be secured by hardening off spring sown plants for putting outside in June, provided the position is sheltered and the soil well drained.

S. sinuata (*S. variabilis*, *S. gloxiniaeflora*) forms a tall branching plant with elegantly marked, colourful, trumpet-shaped veined flowers and lance-shaped leaves.

Many varieties have been selected so that it is possible to obtain separate colours and excellent mixed strains. Superbissima Mixed produces compact large flowered plants. A remarkable F.1 hybrid strain known as 'Splash', forms bushy specimens with many flowers in a wide colour range.

$1\frac{1}{2}$–$2\frac{1}{2}$ ft. Spacing 12 in. May–June in greenhouse. H.H.A.
July–September outdoors.

Salvia. From a Latin word meaning I heal or safe, a reference to the medicinal qualities of certain species. Sometimes known as sage or clary, this is a very large genus containing both annual and perennial species many of which come from California and tropical America, although there are a few of European origin.

Seed of the majority needs sowing in heat early in the year. Germination is often slow and erratic, especially if a fairly warm temperature is not maintained—around 65°F seems to be ideal. If at least 60°F is not possible do not sow before March. Prick off the seedlings into boxes and for best results the next move should be to pots, increasing the size of these according to growth. From the larger pots, move the plants to outdoor positions at the end of May or early June—after hardening off. As necessary take out the growing points to encourage bushy growth.

S. carduacea is a distinct species forming a rosette of thistle-like greenish leaves, well armed with spines. Sometimes known as the

Thistle Sage, it produces heads or whorls of lavender flowers. This species can be sown outdoors in spring or autumn.

S. columbariae is another salvia with whorls of bright blue flowers but needs sowing under glass.

S. farinacea although perennial is more often treated as an annual. It produces long spikes of violet blue flowers and has a number of good forms such as Blue Bedder and Royal Blue, both with deep blue flowers, and Alba, white.

S. grahami (microphylla) is also grown as an annual having crimson blooms, while some variations bear white, purple or carmine flowers.

S. horminum is deservedly popular for sowing directly into flowering positions. Its decorative value lies in the colourful bracts surrounding the tiny flowers. A number of different varieties are available with bracts of pink, purple, blue and white, all being valuable for indoor display.

S. splendens is the well known scarlet sage from Brazil and the original species from which all the well known scarlet bedding salvias have been developed. The stout branching stems bear many showy flower spikes. The type species as well as some of the varieties are inclined to be rather late flowering, meaning a short life when they are used for summer bedding. Some of the named hybrids now available are earlier flowering. They include 'Blaze of Fire', one of the dwarfer sorts, 'St John's Fire', 'Fireball' and 'Harbinger', all with long spikes of brilliant scarlet. 'Tetra Red', is a newer scarlet variety of robust habit. 'Pink Rouge' and 'Purple Blaze' are of the same habit as Blaze of Fire.

Several really dwarf forms growing only 6–9 in are also available. 1–2½ ft. Spacing 10–15 in. July–October. H.H.A.

Sanvitalia. This is a Mexican plant named after the Italian noble family Sanvitali. A useful annual for the front of the border or the rock garden, it is sometimes known as the Creeping Zinnia. Seed can be sown in spring in flowering positions or this subject can be given half-hardy treatment.

S. procumbens has yellow ray petals with a deep purple central disc. There is a form known as *flore plena* with double flowers which remains showy longer. Both are worthy of wider cultivation.

6 in. Spacing 10–12 in. Trailing. August–October. H.H.A.

Saponaria. The common name of this plant—Soapwort—gives a clue to its Latin title which is *sapo*, meaning soap, in reference to the thick juice which comes from the plants and which makes a lather with water.

Seed can be sown in spring or autumn where the plants are to flower. There are two distinct annual species both of European origin.

S. calabrica is a useful dwarf plant of neat habit, first class for edging purposes, especially since it is early flowering usually beginning to show colour in May. The bright pink flowers are freely produced. There are forms known as *Compacta alba*, white, and scarlet.

6–9 in. Spacing 6 in. May–August. H.A.

S. vaccaria (*Lychnis vulgaris*) is sometimes known as Cowherb. An excellent plant for cutting it has sprays of rose pink flowers. A form known as *rosea*, has rather larger heads but it is 'Pink Beauty' which is most widely grown, being free flowering and of better colour. There is also a white variety known as *alba*. All are useful for mixing with other cut flowers.

2–3 ft. Spacing 9–12 in. April–September. H.A.

Saxifraga. This title is said to be derived from two Latin words meaning rock (or stone) and I break, probably because certain species will grow in stony places, while some authorities believe that the name has some medicinal reference. Nearly all members of this large family, which comes chiefly from the Northern Temperate and Arctic regions are perennials, but one or two are of annual habit.

They can be sown in autumn or spring and once established, they usually seed themselves, so that young plants appear annually. They are excellent for the rock garden, front of the border, or moist positions such as the surrounds of a pool.

S. cymbalaria has glossy green, ivy-like foliage which becomes marked with brown, and deep yellow flowers.

S. huetiana is very similar but is inclined to have a more lax habit of growth.

4–6 in. Spacing 6–7 in. May–August. H.A.

Scabiosa. The Latin for this name is *scabies*, meaning itch supposedly in reference to the plant's properties used in curing this disease. It has several common names including Sweet Scabious and Pincushion Flower. There are many species, natives of Europe and Mediterranean districts. Any good soil suits these plants but they do best in sun. As far as possible, they should be grown in sheltered positions for if in open, exposed places, they need light supports. Not only are they attractive when growing in the garden but they are valuable for cutting, having long wiry stems and the flowers being long lasting.

While they are often treated as hardy annuals, seed being sown in flowering positions in the spring for blooming from late August onwards, they can be sown in warmth in late March. After being hardened off in the usual way, they can be placed in flowering positions about mid May. They will then flower early in August and go on until frosts cut them down.

S. atropurpurea is the old fashioned species with well divided leaves and heads of pincushion-like flowers of purple, rose or white. Many varieties have been introduced by seedsmen from Britain, America and other countries. These include the following: 'Azure Fairy', 'Cherry Red', 'Fire King' and 'King of the Blacks'. A separate group has also been produced by hybridists, the flowers having cone-shaped centres. Among these are: 'Blue Cockade', 'Lavender Moon', 'Rose Cockade' and 'White Cockade'.

There are also a number of dwarf sorts in several good colours.

24–30 in. Spacing 9–15 in. August–October. H.H.A.

Schizanthus. This is another plant which owes its name to two Greek words *schizo* and *anthos* meaning cut and flower, obviously a reference to the shape of the petals as a result of the calyx being 'cut'. Of South American origin, this plant was for long considered solely as a greenhouse subject, for pots or border but it will also succeed as a garden plant either from a direct sowing in the open ground in May or from seed sown under glass in March, the plants being hardened off for planting out in late May or early June.

S. grahamii is a tallish plant with rose flowers marked yellow and purple. It has white and pink forms.

S. pinnatus (*hybrida*) is of garden origin and several good strains are now available such as 'Dr Badger's hybrids' and *Wisetonensis*. These take in an extremely wide colour range with exotic markings. A strain known as 'Angel Wings' forms compact, conical plants, the freely produced flowers almost hiding the foliage. Dwarf Monarch mixed, which has flowers in many colours is particularly valuable for pot work. Both of these grow about a foot high.

$1\frac{1}{2}$–$2\frac{1}{2}$ ft (except Dwarf). Spacing 12–15 in. July–September. H.H.A.

Schizopetalon. The deeply incised petals account for this Greek name. Seed can be sown in late April or May, choosing a warm sunny spot where the plants are to bloom. Thin sowing is advisable, since the seedlings do not transplant well. It is helpful if the rather slender plants are supported with twiggy sticks. Some gardeners sow in pots and transplant in early June without disturbing the roots.

S. walkeri from Chile, has deeply cut, white flowers which are delicately fragrant in the evenings. It is for this quality alone that the plants are worth growing. Little patches in the border or rock garden are appreciated, while plants near a living room window, will be noticed because of their pleasing fragrance.

9–12 in. Spacing 4–5 in. July–September. H.A.

Sedum. Best known as Stonecrop, the Latin title means to sit, from the way in which the plants hug or attach themselves to rocks and walls. The majority of the species are perennial but one or two are annuals. These plants are excellent for sunny situations in the rock garden, between paving stones or in selected positions in the front of the border.

S. caeruleum from Mediterranean regions, has bright green, rounded, longish fleshy leaves which as they grow older, become tinted with red. The clusters of blue flowers have a whitish centre. These flowers produce very many tiny seeds which usually become distributed by wind and rain.

S. pilosum is a biennial but is often grown as an annual having grey-green hairy foliage and heads of soft pink flowers.

3–4 in. Spacing 4–6 in. June–August. H.A.

Senecio. This is the title of a very large family of hardy and half-hardy plants, some being regarded almost as weeds. The name itself comes from the Latin *senex* meaning old man probably referring to the fact that many of the seeds have a hairy, whitish pappas appearance. Many species come from South Africa and are best treated as half-hardy annuals, although seed can be sown in flowering quarters early in May. September-raised plants flower much earlier. The single flowered species resemble cineraria which belongs to the same family. Sunshine and good, well drained soil leads to best results. *S. arenarius* has single rosy lilac flowers while there is a mixed strain with a good colour range.

S. elegans is often catalogued as *Jacobea elegans* with the common name of Purple Ragwort. The single reddish-purple flowers have a yellow centre. There is also a mixture taking in a good range of colour. It is the double mixed that is most popular, the colours embraced including crimson, mauve, pink and white. A number of dwarf forms are also occasionally available.

15–18 in.   Spacing 12–15 in.   July–October.   H.H.A.

Shirley Poppy. See *Papaver*.

Silene. This name comes from the Greek *sialon* meaning salve, a sticky liquid which the leaves of some species exude. This accounts for the common name of Catchfly. The subject is best sown where the plants are to flower, the seedlings being thinned so that they have room to develop properly. *S. anglica* is the fairly common pink flowered species, sometimes referred to as Rose Campion. There is also a white form. *S. armeria* is known as Sweet William Catchfly.

Silybum. This is an ancient Greek name given to a group of thistle-like plants. In spite of their appearance, they are very ornamental when placed in the right positions at the back of the border or among shrubs, while they are ideal for the wild garden. They grow well in all soils and seem to prefer a sunny situation. Seed can be sown in March or September. It is also possible to sow in June, treating the plants as biennials for flowering the following year.

S. marianum (*carduus*) has the common names of Milk Thistle, Blessed Thistle and St Mary's Thistle. A native of Mediterranean areas, it forms flat rosettes of large glossy green, marbled white, sometimes up to 18 in long and 6–8 in across. From the centre, strong stems arise carrying heads of rosy-purple flowers. These have a faint sweet scent and are surrounded by pricky bracts. Some growers prevent the flower heads from maturing believing that such action improves the colour of the foliage.

2–3½ ft.   Spacing 2 ft.   July–September.   H.A.

Solanum. This large family, natives of tropical and temperate regions, is said to contain over 1,000 annual and perennial species. The name comes from the Latin *solar*, probably because of the supposed sedative qualities of certain species. All like fairly rich, well drained soil and plenty of sun. Among the perennials *S. capsicastrum*, the Winter Cherry, is one of the best known Christmas pot plants. Even this is often treated as an annual for the greenhouse, seed being sown in February and the plants discarded after the berries wither.

The half-hardy species are raised under glass in the usual way, the hardy annuals, which are not well known, being sown where they are to flower.

S. citrullifolium, a hardy annual from Mexico has rather prickly foliage and spikes of saucer-shaped, violet blue flowers. *S. cornutum* has clusters of yellow flowers often followed by small prickly fruit.

Of the half-hardy species, *S. heterodoxum* has well lobed, hairy leaves and bright blue flowers succeeded by round fruit which eventually turn to greenish-black. *S. pseudo-melongena* is without spines. The greenish flowers are usually followed by berries which ultimately turn red.

2–3 ft. Spacing 12 in. July–September. H.A. and H.H.A.

Specularia. Often known as Venus's Looking Glass, this is a charming annual from South America and the Mediterranean regions.

Viscaria mixed

The name is derived from the Latin, *speculum*, a mirror, a reference to the appearance of the flower. Easily grown and very free flowering, they look well used as edgings, in the rock garden and other prominent places. Sow seed in April where the plants are to flower and so long as the soil is on the light side they will usually sow themselves freely, so that once planted in the garden, seedlings come up annually.

S. *pentagonia* has violet purple flowers rather larger than *S. speculum*. (*Campanula speculum*) which produces its small, bell-shaped, deep violet-blue flowers in great profusion is sometimes obtainable in a white form.

9–12 in. Spacing 6 in. July–September. H.A.

Sphenogyne. See *Ursinia.*

Star of Veldt. See *Dimorphotheca.*

Statice. See *Limonium.*

Stock. See *Matthiola.*

Tagetes. This title is derived from a mythical Etruscan diety and is the proper name for the plants we usually refer to as African and French Marigolds. There is some uncertainty as to why they are so called, since they originate from the American continent. All are easily raised as half-hardy annuals being planted in their flowering positions in May. Alternatively, seed can be sown in the open ground in early May, although it is wise to do this only in soil in an unexposed sunny position. Keep the faded flowers pricked off and the plants will go on flowering for many weeks.

During recent years, seed firms in several countries, and particularly the U.S.A., have devoted much attention to the development of these flowers. To-day, there are many excellent varieties of both types. One reason why African marigolds are not used much as cut flowers is that their foliage is strongly scented. This does not matter unless the flowers are needed for cutting. It is a drawback gradually being overcome, and there are already one or two varieties with odourless foliage.

The early strains of the Africans always produced a proportion of single blooms, but modern sorts produce double flowers only, while the shape of the blooms has been developed and refined.

T. *erecta*, although known as the African Marigold, comes from Mexico and varies in height from 12 in–3 ft. The large rounded flowers are usually fully double and withstand adverse weather conditions. Among the separate named varieties are:

Dwarfs—'Spun Gold', chrysanthemum-flowered of uniform habit. 'Moonshot' clear bright yellow. 'Apollo', a giant-flowered gold. 'Gay Ladies', forming bushy compact plants with fully double large blooms in yellow, orange and golden shades. Tall varieties— 'Doubloon', light yellow. 'Sovereign', golden yellow. 'Lemon Alldouble'. 'Diamond Jubilee', bright yellow, intensely double.

T. patula also from Mexico, is the French Marigold! These are divided into several classes such as Dwarf French Carnation flowered,

Verbena aubletia hybrids

Dwarf French double and Dwarf French single, all with separately named varieties in a good colour range, many having beautifully laced flowers such as bright chestnut red, edged golden yellow and 'Fiesta', crimson-edged yellow. These vary in height from 6–12 in.

Specially good are the following: Carnation flowered, 'Bolero' and 'Carmen'; Dwarf Double, 'Orange Nugget' and 'Marionette' mixed; and Dwarf Single, 'Eliza' and 'Naughty Marietta'.

T. signata (*tenuifolia*) is the species often referred to simply as tagetes. It is ideal for use as an edging plant having finely cut foliage. The plants simply smother themselves with yellow flowers. The form known as pumila is an improvement of the type as are the varieties 'Golden Gem' and 'Carina', while 'Red Carpet' has deep mahogany red flowers.

6 in–3 ft. Spacing 6–12 in. July–October. H.H.A.

Thelesperma. A native of Texas the name of this little known hardy annual is given in reference to the tiny protuberances which appear on the seeds, the name literally meaning warty seed.

Sometimes known and catalogued as *Cosmidium*, the flowers are not unlike those of calliopsis. Seed should be sown in April where the plants are to bloom. For preference, select a sunny well drained site. In such a position the plants are very continuous flowering. In very exposed or windy situations light supports are helpful in keeping the stems upright.

T. burridgeanum produces long stemmed flowers of golden yellow, the centres being attractively marked rich brown. A good border plant, this is an excellent subject for cutting. The finely cut basal foliage is highly decorative.

There are one or two named forms including 'Orange Crown' with rich yellow flowers having brown central markings.

1½–2 ft. Spacing 12–14 in. July–September. H.A.

Thunbergia. Named in honour of Karl Thunberg, a Swedish botanist of the eighteenth century, this is strictly speaking a genus of tender perennial plants. Because of their rapid growth, a few of these are regularly and successfully grown as half-hardy annuals. Seed should be sown in the greenhouse in early spring, the seedlings being moved to small pots when big enough to handle. Later they can be moved to bigger pots or tubs or directly into their greenhouse position where they are to flower. In warm sheltered situations, they can be used outdoors for covering short trellis-work while they are useful for hanging baskets.

T. alata from tropical Africa is known as Black Eyed Susan, having attractive heart-shaped leaves and flattish five lobed flowers of cream or pale orange with a purple-black patch. There are several forms of this species including white and deeper and paler shades of yellow all with a dark centre.

T. gibsonii is persistent flowering with orange-yellow flowers.

2–5 ft. Climbing or trailing. July–October. T.A. or H.H.A.

Tithonia. A name derived from Tithonus who in Greek mythology, was loved by the Goddess Aurora. This plant from Mexico and South America, is an easily grown decorative half-hardy annual.

Sow under glass in March placing the young plants outdoors at the end of May. Useful subjects for the back of the border, they flourish in warm sheltered positions where the soil is on the light side.

T. speciosa (rotundifolia) has mulberry-like foliage and large orange-scarlet flowers about 3 in in diameter. It is variable in height which in fact ranges from 3–6 ft. A form known as Torch having orange-vermilion flowers, rarely grows more than 3 ft. Often known as the Mexican Sunflower, it is the best for garden display.

3–6 ft. Spacing 15 in. August–October. H.H.A.

Tolpis. A French naturalist is said to be responsible for the name of this subject which came into general cultivation in the early seventeenth century. It does well in ordinary soil, preferably in a sunny position. Sow in April where the plants are to flower.

T. barbata, sometimes known as *Crepis barbata*, comes from South Europe and freely produces rosette-like, golden yellow flowers. It is occasionally referred to as the Yellow Garden Hawkweed.

12–15 in. Spacing 9–12 in. July–October. H.A.

Torenia. Named after Olaf Torens, a Swedish Churchman, who is said to have discovered one of the species while travelling in China. This is an excellent free-flowering plant for the cool greenhouse. Seed should be sown in warmth in spring, pricking off the seedlings early and later moving them to pots according to growth. It is helpful if inconspicuous supports are provided while the plants are still small. This ensures they remain shapely. The flowers are somewhat like those of the antirrhinum. *T. asiatica* has dark purple flowers with a white lower lip.

T. fournieri is easily the best known species. The main colouring is of pale violet, the lower three lip petals being deep violet-blue, while the throat is blotched golden-yellow. There are several forms such as *grandiflora* large flowering, and 'The Bride', a pink and white variety. It is the way these markings are placed that have given this species the common name of Wishbone Flower.

12 in. Spacing 12–14 in. July–October. G.A.

Trachymene. Natives of Australia and Borneo, the name in Greek means rough membrane, a reference to the appearance of the seeds. Seed should be sown in warmth in March and grown in pots for greenhouse decoration or seedlings may be planted outdoors in groups selecting a warm position where the soil is on the light side and well drained. *T. caerulea* is sometimes catalogued as *Didiscus coeruleus* and has the common name of Blue Lace Flower which is a good description. It forms clusters of long stemmed, tubular lavender blue flower heads which are useful for cutting.

12–24 in. Spacing 10–12 in. July–October. H.H.A.

Trichosanthes. This is one of the many interesting climbing gourds. A native of India it is cultivated in many tropical places. The name when interpreted from the Greek, means hair or hairy flowers from the appearance of the fringed corolla of each flower.

Seeds are best sown singly in pots, the seedlings being given more room as they grow. They can be cultivated in the cool greenhouse where there is room for such climbers and they should succeed if planted outdoors in June in warm sunny positions, where the soil is rich and where they are given plenty of water especially during dry weather.

T. anguina is known as the Snake or Serpent Gourd. It produces strong hairy stems with tendrils and quite large foliage. The long stemmed flowers are usually produced plentifully, individual plants being male or female, the latter being easily identifiable by the tiny embryo fruit behind the petals. Hand pollination greatly assists the production of the snake-like fruits which when ripe, are greenish white and anything from 1–3 ft long.

Climbing or trailing. Spacing 2 ft. August–September fruiting. H.H.A.

Trifolium. This is one of the many forms of clover or trefoil. Many of these species of European origin are perennials, but one or two are annuals, and suitable for growing in selected places. The name means three leaf from the fact that most species have leaves divided into three parts.

Seed can be sown in spring in sunny borders, places in the rock garden, or around certain shrubby plants that may have grown leggy. *T. incarnatum* has the typical reddish pink flowers of clover and in the right position can be quite an ornamental subject.

12–15 in. Spacing 10–12 in. June–September. H.A.

Tripteris. Native of South Africa, it is only about 50 years ago that this subject came into general cultivation. The name means three winged, a reference to the shape of the seed. They grow well in ordinary good soil in a sunny position. In the afternoons, the flowers appear to fold up, but open fully again the following morning. *T. confusa (osteospermum)* has yellowish-orange flowers with a dark central disc.

T. hyseroides, 'Gaiety' has only recently been introduced. Excellent for bedding it should be sown in small clumps or drifts and throughout the summer it produces many orange flowers up to 2 in in diameter. These have strong slender stems and deep green, scented foliage.

1½–2 ft. Spacing 12 in. June–October. H.H.A.

Tropaeolum. This title came from the Greek word for trophy because the leaves are of shield-like appearance while the flowers resemble a helmet. In ancient times, both of these items were thought of as battle trophies. Better known as Nasturtium and sometimes as the Great Indian Cress, native of South America, they have long enjoyed popularity as easy to grow colourful plants which will brighten up dark corners and unsightly spots as well as proving highly ornamental in prominent places. They flourish in poorish soils. In fact, given rich ground, the plants make too much leafy growth which they may also do in a wet season. Seed can be sown in spring or autumn.

Occasionally, black fly settles on the plants but if dealt with before it gains a hold, it is usually easy to eradicate by using a derris-based insecticide and destroying any nearby weeds on which blackfly often breeds.

T. canariense. See *T. peregrinum*.

T. lobbianum. See *T. peltophorum*.

T. majus is the climbing nasturtium, a vigorous grower producing flowers in a wide colour range. It is from this species that the other groups of nasturtiums have been derived. Although climbing nasturtiums are now usually offered in mixture, separate colours are sometimes available including orange, scarlet, and creamy white, while one or two varieties have very dark foliage.

T. majus nanum is often known as Tom Thumb and varieties rarely exceed 9 or 10 in in height. Here again, the mixtures are mostly grown, but there are good named sorts such as Aurora, apricot; Empress of India, crimson-scarlet with dark leaves; Ryburgh Perfection, scarlet with variegated foliage; and Vesuvius, salmon-rose, dark green leaves.

Of more recent introduction are the double forms of nasturtium. These are divided into two groups, the Globe or dwarf forms which make compact plants 7 or 8 in high, and the Gleam or semi-tall sorts which have runners 12–15 in long, and are useful for hanging baskets, most flowers being scented. Colours available in the Gleam section include yellow, orange, scarlet and salmon.

Lilliput nasturtiums grow only about 6 in high and make neat compact bushy little plants, in a mixture of colours.

T. minus is a dwarf species rarely more than 12 in high, having orange-yellow flowers. It has probably had some influence on the development of the larger Tom Thumb varieties.

T. peltophorum (lobbianum) is sometimes known as Lobb's climbing nasturtium having orange-red flowers with foliage on the small side. Occasionally other colours are available. It was once used quite a lot as a summer climber.

T. peregrinum (canariense) is the Canary Creeper, notable for its attractive foliage and prettily fringed yellow flowers. It will grow well in sun or semi-shade and responds to good treatment and can in fact, be cultivated successfully in quite rich soil without growth becoming coarse.

Variable–climbing. Spacing 6–12 in. June–October. H.A.

Ursinia (*sphenogyne*). This name commemorates John Ursinus, a botanist of the seventeenth century. They are very showy plants of South African origin, having graceful foliage and daisy-like flowers. Unlike many similar South African daisies, the flowers remain open throughout the day. For best results these plants should be grown in well drained soil on the light side and they like plenty of sun. Sow the seed thinly in trays or boxes in the cool greenhouse. Ursinias also can be cultivated as pot specimens, while they can be planted outdoors in June after being hardened off.

U. anethoides has finely cut foliage and strong, wiry stems carrying flowers of rich orange-yellow, each with a purplish central zone. A variety known as Sunstar is not quite so tall growing, the orange-scarlet flowers having a maroon centre.

U. pulchra is a handsome dwarf species producing many showy rich orange flowers with a black zone. *U. pygmaea* is probably the dwarfest of all and very useful for the rock garden as is its form 'Brilliance', both having zoneless orange flowers.

6–15 in. Spacing 9–12 in. July–September. H.H.A.

Venidium. Often known as the Namaqualand Daisy, the explanation of this name is obscure or unknown. A native of South Africa this is among the most brilliant of annual plants. While seed may be sown in May where the plants are to flower, so long as the site is sunny and the soil well drained, it is best to start the seed under glass and plant out the seedlings in late May or early June. Outdoor sowings are doubtful in germination and many gardeners sow in small pots to avoid root disturbance at planting out time. For spring flowering under glass, seed should be sown in August or September, germinating it in a cold frame and moving the seedlings to the cool greenhouse in late September, a winter temperature of 50–55°F being quite suitable. Little water is needed during the winter. By early March the plants should be in their 5 in size flowering pots. Venidiums make excellent cut blooms. Unfortunately many of the flowers have a habit of closing up during dull weather.

V. calendulaceum. See *V. decurrens.*

V. decurrens is a useful garden plant of spreading habit. It has deeply lobed leaves and freely produces large golden yellow flowers which are paler around the central black disc.

V. fastuosum is sometimes known as Monarch of the Veldt. It produces extra large, daisy-like flowers of brilliant orange with a purple black centre. The foliage and flower stems are covered with white downy hairs, the blooms closing during dull light. Given a dry, sunny situation the plants will produce their long stemmed flowers in abundance. *V. fastuosum hybrids* are now offered by all the leading seedsmen. These have a wide colour range including yellow, orange and terra cotta, all with a maroon ring surrounding the shining dark centres.

V. macrocephalum is not very well known. The large lemon-yellow flowers have a glistening dark central disc.

2–2½ ft. Spacing 10–14 in. July–September. H.H.A.

Venus's Looking Glass. See *Specularia*.

Verbena. This is reckoned to be an old Celtic name used by Pliny for one of the species known as ferfain or vervain. Almost all verbenas species are perennials but many of the hybrids are now raised from seeds and treated as annuals. These plants have many uses, not only in the border, but in the rock garden, as edgings and in hanging baskets, window boxes and tubs. Seed can be sown in warmth in February and March, for planting outdoors in May for early flowering, or in April, when less warmth is needed for later blooming.

These plants flourish in good fertile soil and a sunny position and once they have made a good root system, they are able to withstand quite dry conditions.

V. aubletia (canadensis) is a valuable species easily grown as a half-hardy annual. It produces heads of rosy-lilac flowers and there are several forms, including *compacta grandiflora*, with larger flowers and of a more compact habit of growth, and *atroviolacea*, rich violet flowers.

V. hybrida is the best known of the garden types having many different forms. They are usually grouped into three sections, small flowered, giant flowered and the compact or bushy forms.

In the first section there are many auricula eyed varieties including a mixed strain listed as Royal Bouquet. The *grandiflora* or large flowered group is represented by well known varieties such as 'Ellen Willmott', salmon rose but variable; 'Lavender Queen' (or Glory) and 'Scarlet Queen'. The dwarf compact section takes in 'Fireball', scarlet; 'Salmon Queen'; 'Sparkle', scarlet and 'Violet Bouquet'.

Dwarf 9–12 in. Others 12–24 in. Spacing 10–15 in. July–October. H.H.A.

Vicia. This is the classical name of the plants often known as the Tare or tufted Vetch. Many species grow wild in various parts of the world including Britain. They are quite useful as ornamental, semi-climbing plants for odd corners or for growing as something not requiring any attention. Sow seed in growing places in April.

V. cracca has racemes of bluish purple flowers while there is a form with deeper blooms.

3–4 ft. Spacing 15 in. June–August. H.A.

Vinca. Although the origin of this title is uncertain, it probably comes from a Latin word *vinculum* meaning a band, an allusion to the longish tough shoots of this plant. The cultivated vincas are not to be confused with the well known hardy periwinkle *V. difformis*, since some are quite attractive as greenhouse pot plants, while they can

Ornamental Grasses

be started in warmth in April for planting outdoors in warm sheltered places in early June.

V. rosea has large rose coloured flowers with darker centres, while the variety known as 'Little Bright Eye' is white with a red eye, and the 'Little Mixture Strain' takes in several pretty colours.

12 in.   Spacing 9–12 in.   July–September.   T.A. or H.H.A.

Violet Cress. See *Ionopsidium.*

Vipers Bugloss. See *Echium.*

Virginian Stock. See *Malcolmia.*

Viscaria. See *Lychnis.*

Waitzia. This little known family of plants was named in honour of F. M. Waitz, a Javanese doctor and writer. Native of Australia, these showy plants are useful grouped in the mixed border, although it is chiefly for their 'everlasting' flowers that they are cultivated. They prefer soil on the light side and a sunny position. Sow seed in warmth in March and gradually harden off seedlings in the usual way for planting outdoors in early June.

W. aurea is a showy plant with pointed leaves and sprays of golden yellow flowers. *W. grandiflora* is similar but of superior appearance.

W. steetziana is white, sometimes shaded very pale yellow.

12–24 in.   Spacing 9–15 in.   July–September.   H.H.A.

Xanthisma. This unusual name comes from the Greek meaning dyed yellow, a reference to the colour of the flowers. An attractive plant, useful for sowing in patches in the border. Seed can also be sown in warmth, the seedlings being moved to their flowering quarters in May. A light soil on the dry side and a sunny position suits this subject.

X. texanum is sometimes known as Star of Texas. It produces daisy-like yellow flowers up to 2 in diameter, the petals being sharply pointed. Supports may be necessary if the plants are grown in open windy positions.

18–24 in.   Spacing 12 in.   July–October.   H.A. or H.H.A.

Xeranthemum. This is another Greek title meaning dry flower, referring to the dry papery blooms, which is why they are classed among the immortelles or everlastings.

While they are useful when growing in the border, they are cultivated chiefly for their value for decoration in winter. The flowers are useful in posies, while they are sometimes included with fresh flowers for creating a showy display when cut flowers are scarce.

Easily grown, they like the sun and a fairly rich, well drained soil. Seed can be sown in April or early May where the plants are to flower or plants can be raised in the cool greenhouse and moved to flowering positions in May.

X. annuum has silvery foliage and papery purplish-rose flowers (bracts) produced on bushy plants. There is also a double flowering form as well as a mixture of colours.

1½–2½ ft. Spacing 12 in. July–October. H.A.

Zaluzianskya. Sometimes found catalogued under *nycterinia* this half-hardy annual was named in honour of Adam Zaluziansky von Zaluzian, a Polish author of the sixteenth century. These South African plants have the common name of Star Balsam, the flowers being pleasantly fragrant in the evenings.

While seed can be sown outdoors in May in flowering positions where the soil is well drained, they are best started in warmth in March, the seedlings being placed in their flowering positions in May or early June.

Z. capensis has white flowers, the petals being stained deep purple on the outside. The common name of Night Phlox is given because of the time of appearance of the flowers and the fact that they look their best at night.

Z. lychidea is uncommon, the petals being yellow white on the inside and reddish purple on the exterior.

Z. villosa is whitish lilac with a small yellowish centre, the flowers remain open during the day but are more fragrant at night.

9–15 in. Spacing 9–12 in. July–September. H.H.A.

Zea. This is an old Greek name for corn and this subject is included here because of the ornamental effect in the flower garden of the species and varieties which have either variegated foliage or cobs or ears bearing brightly coloured seeds. Cultivated for centuries for its grain, the flower grower will want to cut the cobs for indoor decoration.

Plants are raised as half-hardy annuals by sowing seed in small pots in the greenhouse, moving them to bigger pots as growth proceeds. Seed can also be sown outdoors in warm sunny positions in May, although this means the cobs will be later in developing but the foliage will be ornamental.

Z. mays var. japonica has several forms and the strain offered as quadricolor has variegated foliage in many pretty shades including cream, pink and purple or green. *Z. j. multicolor* has prettily marked foliage and is known as Rainbow Maize, and there is also a less common dwarf form. It is the multicoloured hybrids that are so valued for the great colour variegation of the seeds. The dried cobs are used for indoor decoration, the individual seeds in each cob looking like brightly coloured beads in a riot of colour.

3–4 ft.   Spacing 2 ft.   July–September.   H.H.A.

Zinnia. The name commemorates J. G. Zinn, a professor of botany, who lived early in the eighteenth century. Of Mexican origin, the present day varieties have little resemblance to the original species. This is a reflection on the popularity of the plant which produces such a profusion of flowers. It is the free flowering propensity which has given rise to the common name of Youth and Old Age since the plants continue to flower well over a long period.

Zinnias have the reputation of being a little difficult to raise and there is no doubt that, in their early stages, the plants do need care and attention. Most losses occur through draughts, cold, dampness and poor light. Irregular temperatures are also disliked. Sowings should be made in April in a temperature of 65–70°F. If this is not possible wait until early May, but this will mean later flowering. Sow seed thinly in trays or pans of fine compost. Since the seedlings are subject to damping off disease, sterilised soil is used by many growers. Alternatively, the trays or pans can be watered with a solution of Cheshunt Compound.

Germination is usually quick and as soon as the seedlings are clearly seen, the temperature can be reduced a little. Really thin sowing can do away with pricking off, since this operation often leads to a check in growth. The modern practice of moving the seedlings into soil blocks causes the least disturbance. As far as possible handle them by the seed leaves to avoid damage to the soft stems.

Harden off the seedlings in the cold frame so that by the end of May, they are ready for putting out into the open ground. In the event of the weather being cold or windy, delay planting out until early June. Deeply moved, well drained soil brings best results. The soil should be prepared well in advance of planting time and, wherever possible, well rotted manure or 'ripe' compost and bone meal should be worked in.

Z. augustifolia is also known as *Z. mexicana* and *Z. haageana*. It has single, orange-yellow flowers and from it have come many single and double forms of real merit.

Z. elegans is a species with single, lilac-purple blooms. As a result of hybridisation, an extremely wide colour range has been evolved some flowers having attractively twisted petals. Various named varieties are available.

Reference to the catalogue of specialist growers will show what a large range of named varieties are available. Deserving of mention are Fruit Bowl mixed, a fully double Giant Cactus type; 'Envy', giant double, a lovely chartreuse tone of green; and 'Thumbellina', growing only 6 in high and producing a ball of colour in shades of pink, rose, scarlet, white, orange and gold.

The main flowering period is during August and September. Zinnias are divided into three main groups: (i) the tall large flowered types which are usually disbudded, (ii) the intermediate varieties, (iii) the dwarf growing and small flowered sorts, including the Lilliputs and Tom Thumb types.

The Dahlia flowered, Californian Giants and Burpee Giants are the most popular of the large zinnias, all being available in separate colours as well as mixtures. The Fantasy and Scabious-flowered types are the best of the intermediates. The dwarfer small flowered sorts are more suited to bedding than for cutting and are often known as Lilliput or Pompoms.

It is important to cut the blooms at the right time. This must be when the flowers are just opening.

6 in–3 ft. Spacing 6–15 in. July–October. H.H.A.

Nine

Classified lists of Annuals for special purposes

The following lists of annuals are specially suited to the purposes mentioned. In many cases several varieties may be used and full descriptions will be found under their Dictionary headings. All require the treatment described for general cultivation.

Annuals suitable for autumn sowing

Agrostemma	Gypsophila
Calendula	Iberis
Centaurea	Lathyrus
Echium	Nigella
Gilia	Papaver
Godetia	Saponaria

Annuals for edging

Ageratum	
Alyssum	Mesembryanthemum
Crepis	Nemesia
Gamolepsis	Portulaca
Lobelia	Sanvitalia
Matricaria	Specularia
	Tagetes

Annuals for damp situations

Amaranthus	
Calendula	Nemophila
Helianthus	Nigella
Limnanthes	Perilla
Linaria	Reseda
Linum	Ricinus
	Tagetes

Annuals for dry, sunny positions
Brachycome
Dimorphotheca
Echium
Helipterum
Hibiscus
Mentzelia

Phacelia
Portulaca
Salpiglossis
Ursinia
Venidium
Zinnia

Hardy Annuals for Cutting
Agrostemma milas
Calendula in variety
Centaurea cyanus
Chrysanthemum segatum
Coreopsis (calliopsis)
Godetia in variety.

Gypsophila
Helichrysum in variety.
Leptosyne
Nigella
Reseda (mignonette)
Sweet Peas

Half-Hardy Annuals for Cutting
Callistephus (asters)
Cosmos
Gaillardia
Matthiola (stocks)
Nemesia in variety
Phlox drummondii

Salpiglossis
Statice sinuata
Tithonia
Trachelium
Venidium
Zinnia in variety

Annuals for drying as Everlastings
Ammobium
Gomphrena
Helichrysum

Helipterum
Statice
Xeranthemum

Annuals with coloured foliage
Amaranthus
Atriplex
Centaurea maritima
Chrysanthemum parthenium

Kochia tricophylla
Euphorbia heterophylla
Perilla
Ricinus

Annuals for semi-shady places
Ageratum
Alyssum
Collinsia

Impatiens
Nemophila
Tropaeolum

Annuals for window boxes
Ageratum
Alyssum
Celosia

Petunia
Phlox drummondii
Portulaca

Convulvulus
Echium
Linaria
Lobelia
Matricaria
Malcolmia
Nemophila

Salvia
Specularia
Sweet Peas (dwarf)
Tagetes
Verbena
Vinca (dwarf)
Zinnia (dwarf)

Annuals growing 3–4 ft high
African Marigolds
Cleome
Cosmos
Delphinium (larkspur)
Helianthus
Hibiscus

Malva
Nicotiana
Ricinus
Silybum
Tithonia
Zinnia

Annuals growing under 9 in
Asperula
Downingia
Felicia
Linum
Linaria
Nemesia

Nemophila
Portulaca
Sedum
Ursinia
Viscaria
Virginian Stock

Ornamental Annual Grasses
Agrostis, cloud grass
Aira, hair grass
Avena, animated oat
Briza maxima
Bromus brizaeformis
Coix lachryma

Hordeum jubatum
Lagurus ovatus
Lamarckia aurea
Pennisetum villosum
Tricholaena repens
Zea Maize (coloured)

Annuals with scented flowers
Brachycome iberidifolia
Centaurea moschata
Dracocephalum moldavica
Ionopsidium acaule
Limnanthes douglasii
Matthiola incana

Mentzelia lindleyi
Nicotiana affinis
Reseda odorata
Tagetes lucida
Sweet Peas
Zaluzianskya capensis

Annual Climbers
Colonyction
Eccremocarpus

Quamoclit
Thumbergia

Ipomoea   Tropaeolum majus
Lathyrus, (Sweet Peas)   Tropaeolum peregrinum

Annuals liked by bees

Alyssum maritimum   Echium Blue Bedder
Bartonia aurea   Linaria maroccana
Centaurea (Sweet Sultan)   Nigella damascena
Collinsia bicolor   Phacelia tanacetifolia
Dracocephalum moldavica   Salvia horminum

Sometimes it is desirable to sow beds of separate colours and for this purpose the following can be recommended:

Yellow:

Anthemis   Leptosyne
Argemone   Nasturtium
Calendula   Nemesia
Coreopsis   Tagetes
Dimorphotheca   Tolpis
Gamolepsis   Venidium

White:

Alyssum   Godetia
Antirrhinum   Gypsophila
Asters   Matthiola
Candytuft   Matricaria
Clarkia   Petunia
Cosmos   Zaluzianskya

Red:

Alonsoa   Godetia
Amaranthus   Linum
Anagallis   Nemesia
Clarkia   Salvia
Cuphea   Silene
Eschscholtzia   Viscaria

Blue:

Anagallis   Nemesia
Brachycome   Nemophila
Cornflower   Phacelia
Echium   Specularia
Felicia   Trachelium
Lobelia   Trachymene

Pink:

Agrostemma	Lavatera
Antirrhinum	Malope
Collinsia	Nemesia
Eucharidium	Petunia
Godetia	Saponaria
Iberis	Zinnia

Violet-purple:

Asters	Lathyrus
Centaurea	Matthiola
Clarkia	Nigella
Dianthus	Phlox drummondii
Dracocephalum	Salvia horminum
Gilia	Verbena

Many useful colour schemes can be made by planting half-hardy annuals—plants raised under glass early in the year and planted outside from May onwards.

The following are suggestions for both beds or borders of separate colours or those where several different items are used to provide a showy summer and autumn display.

Blue and lavender shades

- Ageratum
- Aster
- Lobelia
- Nemesia Blue Gem
- Petunia
- Verbena

White and cream shades

- Alyssum
- Lobelia
- Matricaria Silver Ball
- Petunia
- Stocks
- Verbena

Crimson and scarlet shades

- Alonsoa
- Cuphea
- Nemesia
- Petunia
- Phlox drummondii
- Stocks

Orange and yellow shades

- Antirrhinum
- Gamolepsis
- Marigold French
- Marigold African
- Tagetes
- Zinnia

As alternatives to separate colours I have used as a centre piece, French Marigold 'Spry', which has mahogany-red outer petals with a yellow centre. Around this mixed *Phlox drummondii* or mixed petunias edged with *Ageratum* 'Blue Mink'.

An even simpler bed can be made of kochias spaced 2½–3 ft apart, with Gleam nasturtiums used as the ground work. As alternatives to these, mixed petunias or verbenas are effective.

In open situations, beds consisting of one item such as dwarf antirrhinums, bedding dahlias, petunias, Giant Chabaud carnations or dwarf zinnias always attract attention.

It is not essential to stick to the better known half-hardy annuals for summer bedding purposes. Many slightly tender subjects are admirable for planting outdoors from late May onwards, which is usually when beds and borders have been cleared of tulips, daffodils, crocuses, etc. There is no need to do any deep cultivation. The aim should be to clear out all remains of the bulbous crops and to lightly fork over the ground. A little general organic fertiliser or fish manure worked into the surface will be helpful if it is thought the soil needs feeding.

Among reliable if less common plants for summer bedding are the following. *Alonsoa warscewiczii compacta*, scarlet blooms, 12–15 in. Balsam camellia flowered in many pastel shades, 16 in. *Celosia cristata*, Cockscomb, various colours, 10–12 in. *Schizanthus* 'Dwarf Bouquet', many shades, 10–12 in. *Ursinia pulchra aurora*, orange and crimson; cut foliage, 8 in. *Zinnia Thumbelina* mixed. Little plants, 6 in high, covered with double and semi-double flowers—shades of white, yellow, pink, lavender, orange and scarlet.

Any of these subjects can be used in separate beds or planted in little groups in one main bed or border.

Ten

Common Names and Latin Equivalents

African Daisy	*Arctotis*
African Marigold	*Tagetes*
Alkanet	*Anchusa*
Apple of Peru	*Nicandra*
Aster	*Callistephus*
Arabian Primrose	*Arnebia*
Baby Blue Eyes	*Nemophila*
Baby's Breath	*Gypsophila*
Balsam	*Impatiens*
Barberton Daisy	*Gerbera*
Beefsteak plant	*Perilla*
Belvedere cypress	*Kochia*
Bird's Eyes	*Gilia*
Black Eyed Susan	*Rudbeckia*
Black Eyed Susan	*Thunbergia*
Blanket Flower	*Gaillardia*
Blessed Thistle	*Cnicus*
Blue Daisy	*Felicia*
Blue Lace Flower	*Trachymene*
Buckwheat	*Fagopyrum*
Bugloss	*Anchusa*
Burning Bush	*Kochia*
Busy Lizzie	*Impatiens*
Californian Bluebell	*Nemophila*
Californian Poppy	*Eschscholtzia*
Campion	*Lychnis*

Canary Creeper	*Tropaeolum peregrinum*
Candytuft	*Iberis*
Cape Marigold	*Dimorphotheca*
Catch Fly	*Silene*
Chalk Plant	*Gypsophila*
China Aster	*Callistephus*
Chinese Houses	*Collinsia*
Cigar Flower	*Cuphea*
Clock Vine	*Thumbergia*
Corn Cockle	*Lychnis*
Cornflower	*Centaurea*
Corn Marigold	*Chrysanthemum*
Cowherb	*Saponaria*
Cream Cups	*Platystemon*
Devil-in-a-Bush	*Nigella*
Devil's Fig	*Argemone*
Diamond Flower	*Ionopsidium*
Fairy Fans	*Eucharidium*
Fennel Flower	*Nigella*
Fire on the Mountains	*Euphorbia*
Flora's Paintbrush	*Emilia*
Flos Adonis	*Adonis*
Four o'clock	*Mirabilis*
French Marigold	*Tagetes patula*
Golden Cup	*Hunnemannia*
Hawksbeard	*Crepis*
Hypocrite plant	*Euphorbia*
Immortelle	*Xeranthemum*
Italian Pimpernelle	*Anagallis*
Jack-in-the-green	*Nigella*
Jacobaea	*Senecio elegans*
Joseph's Coat	*Amaranthus*
Kingfisher Daisy	*Felicia*
Lablab	*Dolichos*
Lace Flower	*Trachymene*
Lady-in-the-Bower	*Nigella*
Love-in-a-mist	*Nigella*
Love-lies-bleeding	*Amaranthus*

Madwort	*Alyssum*
Mallow	*Malva*
Marigold	*Tagetes*
Marsh Flower	*Alonsoa*
Marvel of Peru	*Mirabilis*
Mexican Fire Plant	*Euphorbia*
Mignonette	*Reseda*
Monkey Flower	*Mimulus*
Nasturtium	*Tropaeolum*
Night Phlox	*Zaluzianskya*
Periwinkle	*Vinca*
Pimpernel	*Anagallis*
Poor Man's Weather Glass	*Anagallis*
Pot Marigold	*Calendula*
Prickly Poppy	*Argemone*
Purslane	*Portulaca*
Rose Campion	*Lychnis*
Rose of Heaven	*Lychnis Coeli rose*
Santa Barbara Poppy	*Hunnemannia*
Sea Dahlia	*Leptosyne*
Snapweed	*Impatiens*
Snow on the Mountain	*Euphorbia*
Star Balsam	*Zaluzianskya*
Strawflower	*Gomphrena*
Summer Cypress	*Kochia*
Sun Plant	*Portulaca*
Swan River Daisy	*Brachycome*
Sweet Pea	*Lathyrus*
Sweet Sultan	*Centaurea*
Tahoka Daisy	*Machaeranthera*
Tassel Flower	*Emilia*
Ten Week Stock	*Matthiola*
Thorn Apple	*Datura*
Tickseed	*Coreopsis*
Tidy Tips	*Layia*
Toadflax	*Linaria*
Tobacco Flower	*Nicotiana*
Touch me not	*Impatiens*

Twin Spur	*Diascia*
Venus's Looking Glass	*Specularia*
Viper's Bugloss	*Echium*
Virginia Stock	*Malcolmia*
Whispering Bells	*Emmenanthe*
Youth and Old Age	*Zinnia elegans*

Index